God's Mighty Warrior™ Devotional Bible

Sheila Walsh

Scripture selections from the
International Children's Bible®

A Division of Thomas Nelson Publishers

NASHVILLE   DALLAS   MEXICO CITY   RIO DE JANEIRO

Dear Mighty Warrior,

Does that title surprise you? Perhaps you don't feel very mighty and you have *way* too many chores or too much homework to have time to be a warrior! The amazing news is that God sees you as a mighty warrior no matter how you feel.

In the Old Testament an angel appeared to a man name Gideon and said to him, "The Lord is with you, mighty warrior!" (Judges 6:12). Gideon could not believe what he was hearing. He told the angel that he was from a family that was no big deal in town; and not only that, but he was the smallest and weakest guy in the bunch! Gideon learned that a mighty warrior is the one who trusts in God, not necessarily the one with the biggest muscles.

Yอน may not know this yet, but being one of God's warriors is the most exciting life offered to any boy on the planet. Whether you are big or small, tough or timid, when God is on your side you are mighty. Gideon discovered that was true. He began to live as the warrior that God made him to be. As he led his men into battle they cried out, "A sword for the Lord and for Gideon!" (Judges 7:20).

I have a son whose name is Christian. It is so awesome to watch him discover who he really is in God's eyes. When he faces tough challenges or tough math we call out, "A sword for the Lord and for Christian!"

You can put your name there too because *you* are God's Mighty Warrior!!

With love and gratitude to God for your life,

Sheila
AKA Christian's Mom

Introduction for Parents

(based on Ephesians 6:10-18)

God created little boys to be mighty warriors…even when they feel small.

Boys are full of energy and imagination. They are (in their minds) the protectors of the fair (their moms and sisters)… guardians of the wild forest (their backyards)…tamers of savage beasts (their pet dog or cat)! Little boys long to be brave and tough…to be Mighty Warriors!

In this storybook Bible format, boys can learn how to be strong, honorable, courageous and true. Selections of actual Bible text from the International Children's Bible® are combined with delightful articles to help a budding "warrior" earn his armor. We hope that your little boy will learn how to be the Mighty Warrior that God created him to be (and capture the heart of his mom)!

Features:

Adventure Quest: articles that encourage a boy's imagination and "quest" for play and adventure, by using games and activities to teach and have fun!

Belt of Truth: articles on values such as honesty, sharing, friendliness, caring and much more.

Guard Your Heart: articles on "Right Living"—basically, manners for boys to learn courtesy, honoring your word, no complaining, etc.

Helmet of Salvation: articles and verses on salvation (sin, or doing things that are wrong, and asking for forgiveness).

Mighty Warriors: Bible heroes that boys will admire and strive to be like.

Shield of Faith: articles to help boys learn how to make right choices (avoiding temptation, obeying your parents, etc.).

Stand Strong: articles on spreading the "Good News of peace," sharing God with your friends, protecting the weak, etc.

Sword of the Spirit: articles that will encourage Scripture memory and the teachings of God.

Table of Contents

Table of Contents *(continued)*

Warrior Favorites

Favorite Colors

_____

_____

_____

_____

_____

Favorite Animals

_____

_____

_____

_____

_____

Favorite Foods

_____
_____
_____
_____
_____

Favorite Toys

_____
_____
_____
_____

Favorite Things to Do

_____
_____
_____
_____

Favorite Games

_____

_____

_____

_____

_____

Favorite Stories

_____

_____

_____

_____

Favorite Bible Verses

_____

_____

_____

_____

God created human beings in his image. In the image of God he created them. He created them male and female. God blessed them and said, "Have many children and grow in number. Fill the earth and be its master. Rule over the fish in the sea and over the birds in the sky. Rule over every living thing that moves on the earth."

God said, "Look, I have given you all the plants that have grain for seeds. And I have given you all the trees whose fruits have seeds in them. They will be food for you. I have given all the green plants to all the animals to eat. They will be food for every wild animal, every bird of the air and every small crawling animal." And it happened. God looked at everything he had made, and it was very good. Evening passed, and morning came. This was the sixth day.

. . . The Lord God put the man in the garden of Eden to care for it and work it.

GENESIS 1:27-31; 2:15

Genesis

Operation Outdoors

Adventure Quest

Have you ever looked at nature and wondered how it all works? Who feeds the birds and teaches them to build nests?

The answer is easy. All of nature is God's creation. He is the one who keeps it all going.

He keeps us going, too. He also has given us a special job in his creation. Before sin entered the world, it was God's perfect plan for Adam to help rule over the earth. He wanted his people to take care of the world he had made. Our job hasn't changed. God wants us to take care of his creation and show love in everything we do.

ACTIVITY

Seed the Need

SUPPLIES:
pinecone
string
peanut butter
bird seed

Want to join God in his work with creation? Now's your chance to help feed the birds that live near your house. Find a large pinecone in your backyard or nearby. Tie a string or piece of yarn to the top of the cone, leaving enough to tie the cone to a branch of a tree. Before you hang it, spread peanut butter all over the cone. Next, sprinkle birdseed over the top of the cone, and press the seeds into the peanut butter. When you're done, find a tree branch near your house where you can hang your pinecone bird feeder. Each day watch to see which birds like your treat.

Treasure Tip

Today you've gotten a taste of the joy that comes from taking care of others. What else can you do to help make the world around you a better place? Ask your parents to suggest ways you can help. Ask God to help you take better care of the people and animals around you.

A mist often rose from the earth and watered all the ground.

Then the Lord God took dust from the ground and formed man from it. The Lord breathed the breath of life into the man's nose. And the man became a living person. Then the Lord God planted a garden in the East, in a place called Eden. He put the man he had formed in that garden.

… The Lord God put the man in the garden of Eden to care for it and work it.

… Then the Lord God said, "It is not good for the man to be alone. I will make a helper who is right for him."

From the ground God formed every wild animal and every bird in the sky. He brought them to the man so the man could name them. Whatever the man called each living thing, that became its name. The man gave names to all the tame animals, to the birds in the sky and to all the wild animals. But Adam did not find a helper that was right for him. So the Lord God caused the man to sleep very deeply. While the man was asleep, God took one of the ribs from the man's body. Then God closed the man's skin at the place where he took the rib. The Lord God used the rib from the man to make a woman. Then the Lord brought the woman to the man.

GENESIS 2:6-8, 15, 18-22

First Forgiveness: Adam

Mighty Warriors

It's easy to remember Adam for his failures. After all, how could he make such a silly mistake as believing a snake? No doubt, Adam really messed up.

But Adam is a hero. He named all the animals. He was given Eve, a beautiful wife. And he walked with God. Being the first man who ever lived is a big deal. It's never easy to be the first anything.

Adam also stands as the first to receive forgiveness. Sin in the world was his fault. But he also looked to God for help.

He admitted his weaknesses. And he humbly received the consequences for his actions. Adam is a mighty warrior because he believed God could get him out of the mess he had created. And he was right. God could and did save Adam. God will also save all people who look to Jesus for hope and forgiveness.

Whenever you sin, remember Adam. Turn to God for help. Admit your sin, and feel the goodness of God's forgiveness.

Warriors

Now the snake was the most clever of all the wild animals the Lord God had made. One day the snake spoke to the woman. He said, "Did God really say that you must not eat fruit from any tree in the garden?"

The woman answered the snake, "We may eat fruit from the trees in the garden. But God told us, 'You must not eat fruit from the tree that is in the middle of the garden. You must not even touch it, or you will die.'"

But the snake said to the woman, "You will not die. God knows that if you eat the fruit from that tree, you will learn about good and evil. Then you will be like God!"

The woman saw that the tree was beautiful. She saw that its fruit was good to eat and that it would make her wise. So she took some of its fruit and ate it. She also gave some of the fruit to her husband who was with her, and he ate it.

GENESIS 3:1-6

Genesis

Enemy Fire

Winning wars would be easy if there were no enemies. You'd just simply march across to the land you want and take it. Unfortunately, life doesn't work that way. Soldiers fight real enemies. If they are not careful, they can be hurt or killed.

We are called God's soldiers for a reason. We are in a great big spiritual battle. We have a very real enemy. Satan has been on earth since God created it. He was in the garden with Adam and Eve. He has been fighting hard against God's people ever since.

Satan is sneaky, but he is not more powerful than God. We can win daily battles against him by standing strong in God's truth. We must watch out for his lies. Ask God to help you know what is true so you can live it and share it with others. God's kingdom grows stronger when his people fight together to believe and live his truth.

Strong

The Lord saw that the human beings on the earth were very wicked. He also saw that their thoughts were only about evil all the time. The Lord was sorry that he had made human beings on the earth. His heart was filled with pain. So the Lord said, "I will destroy all human beings that I made on the earth. And I will destroy every animal and everything that crawls on the earth. I will also destroy the birds of the air. This is because I am sorry that I have made them." But Noah pleased the Lord.

GENESIS 6:5-8

In the Long Run:
Wearing the Belt of Faithfulness

Faithfulness is a really long word. But that's okay. It can help you remember what it means. To be faithful means to keep doing what is right for as long as you live.

Noah was a faithful man. He lived in a place where all the people around him were making bad choices. Everyone else forgot God. But Noah remembered.

He kept his eyes on what God said to do, not on the people around him. Noah's faithfulness pleased God, and God saved the earth through him.

Do you want to be faithful like Noah? Do you want to obey God your whole life? Then tell God what's in your heart. Ask him for help to be faithful. God will be faith-ful to help you!

Truth

ACTIVITY

Take a moment to sing this famous song of praise to God who stays faithful to the end!

Great is Thy faithfulness,
   great is Thy faithfulness,
Morning by morning
   new mercies I see.
All I have needed Thy hand
   hath provided.
Great is Thy faithfulness,
   Lord unto me.

The Lord said to Noah, "I have seen that you are the best man among the people of this time. So you and your family go into the boat. Take with you seven pairs, each male with its female, of every kind of clean animal. And take one pair, each male with its female, of every kind of unclean animal. Take seven pairs of all the birds of the sky, each male with its female. This will allow all these animals to continue living on the earth after the flood. Seven days from now I will send rain on the earth. It will rain 40 days and 40 nights. I will destroy from the earth every living thing that I made."

Noah did everything that the Lord commanded him.

GENESIS 7:1-5

What It's All A-boat

Imagine being a young recruit in the army. One day your commanding officer gives you an order that seems quite strange. He is sending you into enemy territory. He wants you to cover your skin with mud. He tells you to tie branches to your back. Pretty soon, you look rather silly.

Would you obey, or would you be afraid of what your friends think? If you're a smart soldier, you'll do as you're told.

Soldiers can hide better from the enemy when they blend in with their surroundings. It might look strange on a normal day. But when you're trying to sneak through woods and marshes, the covering can save your life. It's a good thing Noah obeyed God, his Commanding Officer. It looked very funny to everyone else for him to be building a boat far from water. However, no one was laughing when the flood came. It's always better to pay more attention to what God says if we want to stay safe.

Treasure Tip

God's directions aren't always easy to follow. But when we obey, we experience God's blessing. What has God asked you to do that you think is too hard? Is it loving your brother or sister? Is it sharing your faith with others? Is it being respectful to your parents? Whatever it is, tell God about it. Ask him to help you obey, no matter what anyone else says or thinks.

A Boatload of Fun

SUPPLIES:
several blankets
flashlights
canteen
food
stuffed animals

Today, you are going to be Noah! God has called you to build a boat and fill it with animals. Using chairs, the bed and the dresser handles, work with your mom or dad to tie blankets into a cave-like boat. Think carefully through what you may need to bring on board.

Pack food for you and the animals. Bring a canteen of water. When everything is inside, have a parent turn off the lights. Pretend that your flashlight is a lantern. Can you imagine living there with the animals for the whole day? A week? How about over 150 days!

The Lord said to Abram, "Leave your country, your relatives and your father's family. Go to the land I will show you.

I will make you a great nation,
 and I will bless you.
I will make you famous,
 And you will be a blessing
  to others.
I will bless those who bless you.
 I will place a curse on those who
  harm you.
And all the people on earth
 will be blessed through you."

So Abram left Haran as the Lord had told him. And Lot went with him. At this time Abram was 75 years old.

…The Lord appeared to Abram. The Lord said, "I will give this land to your descendants." So Abram built an altar there to the Lord, who had appeared to him. Then Abram traveled from Shechem to the mountain east of Bethel. And he set up his tent there. Bethel was to the west, and Ai was to the east. There Abram built another altar to the Lord and worshiped him. After this, he traveled on toward southern Canaan.

GENESIS 12:1-4, 7-9

Field Maneuvers

Adventure Quest

Have you ever gotten lost? It's scary when you don't know where you are or where you're going.

Abraham probably felt a little scared, too. God told him to get up from the land he called home. He told him to leave and travel to a place he had never been. Abraham immediately packed up his belongings. He took his family with him and followed the Lord's orders. When he finally arrived at God's special spot, God appeared to Abraham and promised to bless him for his obedience.

Sometimes it's hard to obey, especially if we don't like it or understand why. God tells us to follow his orders whether we understand his plan or not. Take the faith walk challenge to sharpen your listening skills to hear God's orders.

ACTIVITY

Faith Walk

SUPPLIES:
bandana
hoops, chairs,
blankets to
create tunnels, etc.
candy

Have a parent or sibling set up an obstacle course in the backyard. Feel free to use chairs, hoops, blankets and whatever you can to make the journey an unusual one. Have them tie a bandana around your eyes. Then let them lead you by the hand through the obstacle course. At times, let go of their hand and have them simply speak the direction you should go. When you arrive at the end, treat yourself to a piece of candy.

Treasure Tip

Was it scary having to walk without seeing where you were going? Did your leader do a good job showing the way? Remember that we cannot see God, but he is always there. He will lead us in the right path if we listen for his voice in our hearts and in his Word. We may not always know his whole plan. But we know that if we obey what God tells us, we will find his blessing in the end. Ask God to help you follow him, no matter where he leads!

25

When Abram was 99 years old, the Lord appeared to him. The Lord said, "I am God All-Powerful. Obey me and do what is right. I will make an agreement between us. I will make you the ancestor of many people."

Then Abram bowed facedown on the ground. God said to him, "I am making my agreement with you: I will make you the father of many nations. I am changing your name from Abram to Abraham. This is because I am making you a father of many nations."

GENESIS 17:1-5

Obedient One: Abraham

Do you have a great grandmother or a relative who is really old? Can you imagine how funny it would look for her to have a baby in her old age?

God told Abraham that his 90-year-old wife Sarah was going to have a son. Abraham thought the idea was impossible at first. Then God asked him, "Is anything too hard for me?" Abraham admitted that God can do anything.

Later that year, Sarah had a baby boy. God made millions of descendants come through Abraham's family line, just like he promised.

Abraham was a hero because he believed and obeyed God. When God told him to move to a new country, he did. When he told him to sacrifice his own son, he trusted God to do what was right. Again and again God called Abraham to do amazing things.

Warriors

Abraham believed God would work through him, so he obeyed.

What has God asked you to do as his child? Will you believe that God's way is best like Abraham did? Nothing is impossible with God. Ask him to work in your heart and through your life to please him.

Moses said to Joshua, "Choose some men and go and fight the Amalekites. Tomorrow I will stand on the top of the hill. I will hold the stick God gave me to carry."

Joshua obeyed Moses and went to fight the Amalekites. At the same time Moses, Aaron and Hur went to the top of the hill. As long as Moses held his hands up, the Israelites would win the fight. But when Moses put his hands down, the Amalekites would win. Later, Moses' arms became tired. So the men put a large rock under Moses, and he sat on it. Then Aaron and Hur held up Moses' hands.

Aaron was on one side of Moses, and Hur was on the other side. They held his hands up like this until the sun went down. So Joshua defeated the Amalekites in this battle.

Then the Lord said to Moses, "Write about this battle in a book so people will remember. And be sure to tell Joshua. Tell him because I will completely destroy the Amalekites from the earth."

EXODUS 17:9-14

Exodus

Command Post

Guard Your Heart

It's time for "big church." You know you are faced with one hour of grown-up talk. You choose to:

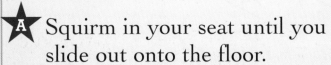
A Squirm in your seat until you slide out onto the floor.

B Keep making groaning sounds until your parents get mad.

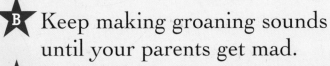
C Sit still and quietly pray and listen for Bible truths you can understand.

D Rattle pieces of paper as you make paper airplanes.

Sometimes God asks us to do things that might seem hard. Moses had to keep his arms held up over his head through a whole battle. You have to sit still at church.

Just like Moses' battle, the church service is very important. You need to stay quiet and still, and listen. Simply think of it as your battle-command post. It's up to you to keep watch and listen! God doesn't ask you to do anything that he won't help you do. Ask him now to give you the strength of Moses the next time you sit through a church service.

God came to Balaam and asked, "Who are these men with you?"

Balaam said to God, "The king of Moab, Balak son of Zippor, sent them. He sent me this message: 'A nation has come out of Egypt. They cover the land. So come and put a curse on them. Then maybe I can fight them and force them out of my land.'"

But God said to Balaam, "Do not go with them. Don't put a curse on those people. I have blessed them."

The next morning Balaam awoke and said to Balak's leaders, "Go back to your own country. The Lord will not let me go with you."

So the Moabite leaders went back to Balak. They said, "Balaam refused to come with us."

NUMBERS 22:9-14

Hold Your Fire!

Guard Your Heart

You were playing with the truck first. The new boy came and, without even asking, grabbed it out of your hands. Now he's playing with it. You decide to:

A Grab it back and yell at him for stealing your truck.

B Start a fist fight and call him names.

C Get another toy and ask him if he'd like to play with you.

D Start crying until the teacher gets it back for you.

35

It's good to remember that every person is a sinner. We all have selfish hearts and want our own way. Even your friends at school. Sometimes they may say or do mean things that make you sad or angry. They may be wrong, but God says that we don't need to get even.

Heart

We can't fix their ugly behavior by being mean, too. Instead, we need to overcome their sin with goodness. Kind words and actions can help others know God better.

The Lord said to Moses, "Phinehas son of Eleazar, the son of Aaron, the priest, has saved the Israelites from my anger. He is like I am in his concern for the people. He tried to save my honor among them. So I will not kill them. So tell Phinehas that I am making my peace agreement with him. He and all his descendants will have an agreement. They will always be priests. This is because he had great concern for the honor of his God. He removed the sins of the Israelites so they would belong to God."

NUMBERS 25:10-13

A Serious Salute

You're hanging out with your buddies. As usual, you are all joking around when it comes time for lunch — and the blessing. Should you:

A Act like you don't remember the blessing and just start eating?

B Say the blessing as silly as you can to see who will laugh?

C Tell someone else to say it?

D Take a moment to thank God for your food and friends?

You don't have to have a long face when you pray. But you do need to realize that praying means talking to the very God who made the universe. He deserves your respect and full attention. And he wants you to be thankful for all he has done for you. God loves it when we honor him by talking to him and about him with a happy heart.

Heart

Our good attitude may actually help the others around us know and honor God better, too. So be on the alert for ways to honor God at home, school, church and even at play. Ask God to help you honor him in all you do.

The people were having a good time at the celebration. They said, "Bring Samson out to perform for us." So they brought Samson from the prison. He performed for them. They made him stand between the pillars of the temple of Dagon. A servant was holding his hand, Samson said to him, "Let me feel the pillars that hold up the temple. I want to lean against them." Now the temple was full of men and women. All the kings of the Philistines were there. There were about 3,000 men and women on the roof. They watched Samson perform. Then Samson prayed to the Lord. He said, "Lord God, remember me.

God, please give me strength one more time. Let me pay these Philistines back for putting out my two eyes!" Then Samson held the two center pillars of the temple. These two pillars supported the whole temple. He braced himself between the two pillars. His right hand was on one, and his left hand was on the other. Samson said, "Let me die with these Philistines!" Then he pushed as hard as he could. And the temple fell on the kings and all the people in it. So Samson killed more of the Philistines when he died than when he was alive.

JUDGES 16:25-30

Supernatural Power: Samson

Mighty Warriors

Want to know who was the strongest man who ever lived? Meet Samson, God's chosen judge for the Israelite people. God chose Samson even before he was born. He put his Spirit on him and gave him supernatural strength. God gave Samson the power to kill thousands of Philistines all by himself.

Samson was strong as long as God was with him. But Samson disobeyed God and became like the enemies he was supposed to fight.

A woman tricked Samson into telling her the secret of his strength. When she cut off his hair, Samson lost his strength. But Samson repented of his sin, and God forgave him. God gave Samson the strength to put an end to the Philistines one last time.

God gives each of us special gifts to use for him. But if we forget about God, we lose our power, too. Ask God to help you stay strong in his power for your whole life.

Warriors

45

This is what the Lord of heaven's armies says: "The Israelites came out of Egypt. But the Amalekites tried to stop them from going to Canaan. I saw what they did. Now go, attack the Amalekites. Destroy everything that belongs to them as an offering to the Lord.

. . . Then Saul defeated the Amalekites. He fought them all the way from Havilah to Shur, at the border of Egypt.

. . . But Saul and the army let Agag live. They also let the best sheep, fat cattle and lambs live. They let every good animal live. They did not want to destroy them. But when they found an animal that was weak or useless, they killed it.

1 SAMUEL 15:2-3, 7, 9-11

1 Samuel

Distract and Trap

Shield of Faith

Saul had done a pretty good job. After all, he had wiped out most of the enemy. So why was God so upset?

Saul had disobeyed orders. He was to take out all of the enemy. Saul got distracted by the money and people he wanted to keep for himself. His bad choice cost him his crown.

God warns all his soldiers to stay on guard. We cannot have any part of Satan's kingdom. We cannot be friends with the world, because the world hates God. It is tempting to want to have a lot of money, the nicest toys, the coolest friends. But watch out! If the people or things of this world make you forget God and his orders, then they are wrong.

Faith

It's a trap. You need to take time out to talk to God. Ask him to remind you about what is important. Then ask him to help you love God and hate sin.

Jesse had seven of his sons pass by Samuel. But Samuel said to him, "The Lord has not chosen any of these."

Then he asked Jesse, "Are these all the sons you have?"

Jesse answered, "I still have the youngest son. He is out taking care of the sheep."

Samuel said, "Send for him. We will not sit down to eat until he arrives."

So Jesse sent and had his youngest son brought in. He was a fine boy, tanned and handsome.

The Lord said to Samuel, "Go! Appoint him. He is the one."

So Samuel took the container of olive oil. Then he poured oil on Jesse's youngest son to appoint him in front of his brothers. From that day on, the Lord's Spirit entered David with power. Samuel then went back to Ramah.

1 SAMUEL 16:10-13

1 Samuel

Young Warrior: David

Mighty Warriors

Do you ever feel like you're too young to do much good for God? If so, take a look at young David and think again.

David was the youngest of all his brothers. He was too little to go to war, so he kept his father's sheep instead. Though David was young, his faith in God was big and strong. He used his time alone in the fields to grow his friendship with God. He prayed and sang to him all the time. God protected David and helped him kill the wild animals that attacked the sheep.

When David learned about the huge giant, Goliath, he wasn't afraid. He knew that Goliath was no match for God. While everyone stood back in fear, David went toward Goliath with full courage. He knew God would help him win. And God did—using only a slingshot and a stone.

David was ready to fight Goliath because he already knew he could trust God. Do you have a close friendship with God, too? Do you talk and sing to him like David? If not, ask God to help you learn to be better friends with him. Ask him to help you be ready to fight evil when the right time comes.

David said to Saul, "Don't let any-one be discouraged. I, your servant, will go and fight this Philistine!"

… He took his stick in his hand. And he chose five smooth stones from a stream. He put them in his pouch and held his sling in his hand. Then he went to meet Goliath.

At the same time, the Philistine was coming closer to David. The man who held his shield walked in front of him. Goliath looked at David. He saw that David was only a boy, tanned and handsome. He looked down at David with disgust. He said, "Do you think I am a dog, that you come at me with a stick?" He used his gods' names to curse David.

… But David said to him, "You come to me using a sword, a large spear and a small spear. But I come to you in the name of the Lord of heaven's armies. He's the God of the armies of Israel! You have spoken out against him."

… As Goliath came near to attack him, David ran quickly to meet him. He took a stone from his pouch. He put it into his sling and slung it. The stone hit the Philistine on his forehead and sank into it. Goliath fell facedown on the ground.

1 SAMUEL 17:32, 40-43, 45, 48-49

Missile Launch

Adventure Quest

If you had to go into battle, what weapon would you choose? Would you look for the newest and most powerful one you could find? Would you look for the best armor for protection?

Most people would. That's why David was so different.

David faced Goliath, the tallest and scariest enemy Israel had ever seen. Even though the king offered his finest armor, David said no. He didn't need to trust in fancy weapons. David knew that God would give him the victory. So David grabbed his shepherd's staff and a sling. Then he chose five smooth stones. With one simple swing of his sling, David shot the stone straight into Goliath's forehead. The giant fell over dead, and David defeated the Philistines.

Target Practice

First, create your target. Set up a row of cans that are different heights on a picnic table or box out in the backyard. Then take 10 giant steps backward, and mark your spot. Without crossing the line, see how many balls it takes to knock down all the cans. If it is too difficult, you can move forward a little. If it's too easy, try moving back some.

Treasure Tip

David knew a secret that the giant Goliath didn't know. When God is for us, no one can fight against us! We don't ever need to be afraid of what other people think. We don't even need to worry about how we are going to protect ourselves. We just need to obey God and stay close to him. He will give us the strength, courage and ability we need to do his work!

When David finished talking with Saul, Jonathan felt very close to David. He loved David as much as he loved himself.

… Jonathan made an agreement with David. He did this because he loved David as much as himself. He took off his coat and gave it to David. He also gave David his uniform, including his sword, bow and belt.

… Saul told his son Jonathan and all his servants to kill David. But Jonathan cared very much for David. So he warned David, "My father Saul is looking for a chance to kill you. Watch out in the morning. Hide in a secret place."

1 SAMUEL 18:1, 3-4; 19:1-2

Lessons in Loyalty:
Wearing the Belt of Love

What makes a man want to become a soldier to fight for others? In a word, it's love. When we love others, we think about their needs more than our own. God says that love is the most important part of life.

Jonathan loved David very much. He promised to stay loyal to him. He risked his own life to save him.

Jesus did even more than that. He loved us so much that he gave his life for us. His death and resurrection saved God's people from their own sin and death. God shows us through Jonathan and Jesus what it means to love. Ask God today to help you love like him.

Truth

ACTIVITY

Jonathan and David made a special agreement to always love each other. You can make a special pact with your mom and dad. Create your own secret handshake, and share it only with your parents. Use it whenever you want to remind them of your love!

David sang this song to the Lord. He sang it when the Lord had saved him from Saul and all his other enemies. He said:

The Lord is my rock, my place of
safety, my Savior.
My God is my rock.
I can run to him for safety.
He is my shield and my saving
strength.
The Lord is my high tower and my
place of safety.
The Lord saves me from those who
want to harm me.
I will call to the Lord.
He is worthy of praise.
And I will be saved from my enemies.

2 SAMUEL 22:1-4

Top Gun

Do you ever let your room get so messy you don't think you could possibly clean it all by yourself? Even impossible tasks look better if you have someone to help you.

God says all of life is a lot like your room. At times, it gets very messy. Often we don't know what to do. We have trouble making good decisions. We need a lot of help to make life right.

God knows we can't fight the fight of faith on our own. He promises to be our steady help. In fact, he says that he has all the supplies we could ever need to live life the right way. But we have to come to him for it. We must see Jesus as our strength and courage that we need for life.

Do you think you can make it through life with a good family and good friends?

Faith

Other people are a blessing. But a relationship with God is what's needed most. Ask him today to help you trust him and love him more.

Elijah answered, "I have not caused trouble in Israel. You and your father's family have caused all this trouble. You have not obeyed the Lord's commands. You have followed the Baals."

. . . Elijah said, "I am the only prophet of the Lord here. But there are 450 prophets of Baal. So bring two bulls. Let the prophets of Baal choose one bull. Let them kill it and cut it into pieces. Then let them put the meat on the wood. But they are not to set fire to it. Then I will do the same with the other bull. And I will put it on the wood. But I will not set fire to it.

You prophets of Baal, pray to your god. And I will pray to the Lord. The god who answers the prayer will set fire to his wood. He is the true God."

. . . Then fire from the Lord came down. It burned the sacrifice, the wood, the stones and the ground around the altar. It also dried up the water in the ditch. When all the people saw this, they fell down to the ground. They cried, "The Lord is God! The Lord is God!"

1 KINGS 18:18, 22-24, 38-39

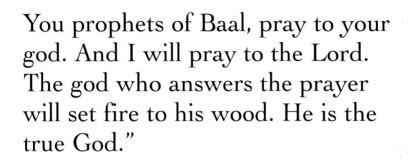

1 Kings

On Guard!

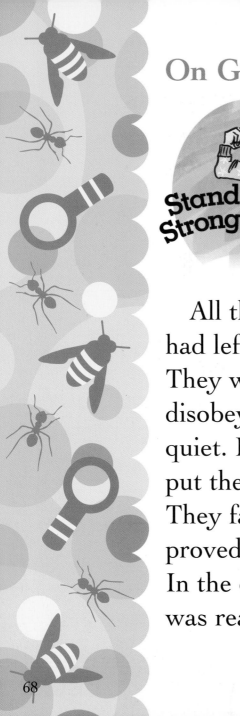

Stand Strong

Imagine one soldier destroying an entire army. Elijah was that one soldier.

All the priests around Elijah had left God to worship idols. They were leading the people to disobey, too. Elijah couldn't keep quiet. He had to stop them. He put their fake gods to the test. They failed in a big way. But God proved himself in a blaze of fire. In the end, everyone knew who was really God.

We need to be like Elijah. It isn't easy to choose God's way when everyone around us is disobeying. But we need to remember that God's way is the only way to blessing. We must stand up for the truth, no matter what our friends say. God will help others see his glory when we remain in the truth. Ask God to make you brave and strong like Elijah.

Strong

Esther sent this answer to Mordecai: "Go and get all the Jews in Susa together. For my sake, give up eating. Do not eat or drink for three days, night and day. I and my servant girls will also give up eating. Then I will go to the king, even though it is against the law. And if I die, I die."

So Mordecai went away. He did everything Esther had told him to do.

ESTHER 4:15-17

Esther

The Right Escape Route

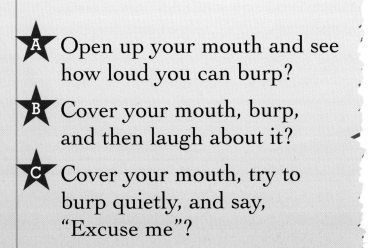

Guard Your Heart

You're sitting at the dinner table and being good. Suddenly you feel that familiar tickle in your tummy. You know it's on its way up. Do you:

> **A** Open up your mouth and see how loud you can burp?
>
> **B** Cover your mouth, burp, and then laugh about it?
>
> **C** Cover your mouth, try to burp quietly, and say, "Excuse me"?

71

It's okay. Burps happen. So do many other bodily noises. But one thing we learn from Esther is the art of asking to be excused. Of course, she was hoping the king would excuse her for coming to his throne without permission. In your case, you simply need to ask those around you to please excuse you. In fact, the words "excuse me" can get you out of all kinds of sticky situations.

Heart

Whenever you need to get away, just use those two magic words. They let others know that you are growing up. It also shows respect for those around you.

Happy is the person who doesn't listen
   to the wicked.
   He doesn't go where sinners go.
   He doesn't do what the bad people do.
He loves the Lord's teachings.
   He thinks about those teachings
      day and night.
He is strong, like a tree planted by a river.
   It produces fruit in season.
   Its leaves don't die.
Everything he does will succeed.

But wicked people are not like that.
   They are like useless chaff
      that the wind blows away.
So the wicked will not escape God's
      punishment.
   Sinners will not worship God with
      good people.
This is because the Lord protects
      good people.
   But the wicked will be destroyed.

PSALM 1:1-6

Secret Strength

Sword of the Spirit

In this exercise you need to find a tree (just imagine one if you can't go outside). Now try to push it over. Try even harder. Did it move at all? Why or why not?

Trees get their strength from their roots. Roots look a lot like the branches, except they go way down into the ground as an anchor for the tree. Even little trees often have a big root system in place.

God wants us to be like the trees he made. He wants us to grow in God's Word. He wants us to trust him and live our lives in complete obedience to the Bible. When we do, we grow really big spiritual roots. Then when hard times come into our lives, we won't be pushed over.

We will hold fast to the truth we know. We will bear fruit that comes with knowing Jesus.

How do your roots look? If you want to grow stronger, start memorizing God's Word today!

Memory Portion

Mind Guard

PSALM 1:2

He loves the Lord's teachings.
He thinks about those teachings
day and night.

The Lord is my shepherd.
I have everything I need.
He gives me rest in green pastures.
He leads me to calm water.
He gives me new strength.
For the good of his name,
he leads me on paths that
are right.
Even if I walk
through a very dark valley,
I will not be afraid
because you are with me.
Your rod and your shepherd's staff
comfort me.

PSALM 23:1-4

Psalms

On Staff

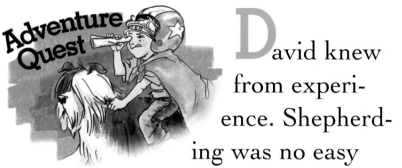

David knew from experience. Shepherding was no easy job. Sheep are always getting into trouble. They can't take care of themselves. They don't even know where they are going. So the shepherd would use his staff (a large walking stick with a hook on the end) to lead them to food. He also used his staff to beat off wild animals and to pick up sheep that had fallen or gone away from the flock.

David said that the Lord was his shepherd. God took care of him, just like David cared for the sheep. God's staff gently guided David to the truth he needed to know for life. God's staff was a comfort to David, because he knew that God loved him. He never needed to be afraid because he knew that his shepherd was standing guard, keeping him safe.

Quest

Stick to It

SUPPLIES:
long stick
markers
strips of fabric
or yarn

Take a hike! Get outside with a parent or guardian and go on a hunt for your own shepherd's staff. Don't bother finding one with a hook. Instead, look for the straightest stick you can find. It should be about as tall as you are or slightly taller.

Once you've found it, bring it back home to make it yours. Use markers to write your name on it. Decorate it with yarn, feathers or anything you want to make it unique. You can even have a parent help you carve in secret markings.

Treasure Tip

Whenever you go on a nature walk, remember to use your staff! You can add new markings whenever you want. Each time you use it, remember that God gently leads you, too. God is your Shepherd who leads you to green pastures and still waters. While you're walking, thank God for being with you. Thank him for his goodness and the protection he gives to his sheep.

You answer us in amazing ways,
God our Savior.
People everywhere on the earth
and beyond the sea trust you.
You made the mountains by your strength.
You have great power.
You stopped the roaring seas,
the roaring waves and the uproar of
the nations.
Even those people at the ends of the earth
fear your miracles.
You are praised from where the sun
rises to where it sets.

You take care of the land and water it.
You make it very fertile.
The rivers of God are full of water.
Grain grows because you make it grow.

PSALM 65:5-9

Nature Nut

Can you see God? Look around outside. Is he there? Don't worry; it's not just you. None of us can see God with our eyes. God the Father is a spirit, and he doesn't have a body like us. So how can we know he is really there?

Look around again. What do you see? Do you see the trees, grass, flowers and birds? Do you see clouds in the sky and the sun shining down? How did what you see get there? Though we can't see God with our eyes, we can see what he has made. Every part of God's marvelous creation shows us how powerful God is. It tells us how wise, creative and loving God is.

Treasure Tip

Many scientists want us to believe that all of creation happened by accident. They don't want us to believe God had anything to do with it. How does the nature you found show a design? Can a good design happen without someone designing it? Take time to thank God for proving his presence through his creation.

ACTIVITY

Nature Hunt

Ask a parent to take you on a nature hunt in your backyard or a hike in the woods. Take along your pad of paper and a pen to record what you find. If you can't write yet, just simply draw a picture of what you see. How many living creatures did you see? How many different kinds of plants?

Feel free to collect leaves, lichen, nuts or other finds from your hunt and place them in your bag. When you get home, glue some of the pieces onto your shoebox to make a nature keeper. Whenever you go on a nature hunt, you can keep your rare finds in your box for later exploration!

SUPPLIES:
notepad and pen
paper (or plastic) bag for collecting
shoebox

Tougher Challenge

Use the chart below to score your nature-finding skills. See which family member scores the most points.

Bird nest	5 pts
Bird	2 pts
Insect	4 pts
Nut	2 pts
Squirrel	2 pts
Lichen	1 pt
Reptile	8 pts
Flower	2 pts
Pinecone	1 pt
Miscellaneous	2 pts

L et God come and scatter his enemies.
Let those who hate him run away.
Blow them away as smoke
   is driven away by the wind,
As wax melts before a fire,
   let the wicked be destroyed
      before God.
But those who do right should
      be glad.
   They should rejoice before God.
   They should be happy and glad.

Sing to God. Sing praises to his name.
Prepare the way for him
   who rides through the desert.

His name is the Lord.
　　Rejoice before him.
God is in his holy Temple.
　　He is a father to orphans.
　　He defends the widows.
God gives the lonely a home.
　　He leads prisoners out with joy.
　　But those who turn against God
　　　　will live in a dry land.

PSALM 68:1-6

Psalms

True Defender

What makes a superhero? Special powers, of course. But every super-hero needs someone to save. Without a cry for help, superheros would have no job to do.

God gives each of his soldiers special strength to do his work. We just need to listen for the cries for help.

God wants his people to pay close attention to widows and orphans. Women who have lost their husbands and children who have lost their parents may feel very sad. They may feel lonely.

They also may have need for money, clothes and even a place to live. We can come to their rescue just like a superhero. We can encourage them through friendship. We can help meet their needs by raising money through a yard sale or lemonade stand, or by asking for grown-ups to help. Ask God to help you be creative in the many ways you can be a true defender for the helpless. Then put your plan into action!

Strong

The Lord shows mercy and is kind.
He does not become angry quickly,
    and he has great love.
He will not always scold us.
    He will not be angry forever.
He has not punished us as our sins
        should be punished.
    He has not repaid us for the evil we
        have done. . . .

The Lord has mercy on those who fear
        him,
    as a father has mercy on his children.
He knows how we were made.
    He remembers that we are dust.

PSALM 103:8-10, 13-14

Psalms

90

Fallen Soldier

Have you ever seen a battle scar? Men who have fought in past wars still have marks that remind them of the fight.

God says that the battle we fight against sin and Satan is hard. We are easily tricked when we forget God's truth and start listening to lies.

If we forget to use our weapons, we will taste defeat. Our hearts get scarred. We fall into the enemy's trap, and we sin against God.

What can a fallen soldier do? Should we give up if we fail in the fight? No! God offers us forgiveness right away whenever we ask him for it. We can face God without fear because he is merciful and kind to us. He has great love for his children.

Faith

We may still suffer the consequences of our bad choices. But the scars can remind us of God's goodness. They can remind us not to make the same mistakes again. God can use even our failures to make us stronger soldiers.

As high as the sky is above the earth,
so great is his love for those who
respect him.
He has taken our sins away from us
as far as the east is from west. . . .

Human life is like grass.
We grow like a flower in the field.
After the wind blows, the flower is gone.
There is no sign of where it was.
But the Lord's love for those who fear him
continues forever and ever.
And his goodness continues to their
grandchildren
and to those who keep his agreement
and who remember to obey his orders.

PSALM 103:11-12, 15-18

Psalms

Go the Distance

Have you ever tried to touch a cloud? Sometimes they seem so fluffy that you could just reach out and take a bite! Really, the clouds are very high up. The sky itself keeps going and going.

God wants us to know how much he loves his kids. He gives us a cool picture of it in Psalms. He says that his love for us is just as big as the distance between the sky and earth!

In other words, his love for us just keeps going and going.

He also says that, because he loves us, he will forgive us when we sin. We just need to admit when we've messed up and ask for forgiveness. He doesn't keep a list of how many times you've failed. Every time you confess your sin, he erases it.

Salvation

He separates it from you so that you never have to think about it again. Like the verse says, he takes it away "as far as the east is from west."

Have you sinned today? Tell God about it. Then thank him for his forgiveness and love.

How can a young person live a pure life?
He can do it by obeying your word.
With all my heart I try to obey you, God.
Don't let me break your commands.
I have taken your words to heart
so I would not sin against you.
Lord, you should be praised.
Teach me your demands.
My lips will tell about
all the laws you have spoken.
I enjoy living by your rules
as people enjoy great riches.
I think about your orders
and study your ways.
I enjoy obeying your demands.
And I will not forget your word.

Psalms

Combat Manual

Sword of the Spirit

Have you ever gotten a cool gift for Christmas that had to be put together before you could play with it? How did your mom or dad know how to fix it? Did they just do what they wanted, or did they read the directions?

God has a very special design for your life, much like that gift. He wants you to be holy, just like he is. He has even included directions for you to follow.

The instructions to living a godly life are found in the Bible. It also tells you how to fight against sin and Satan. As you study and memorize God's Word, your life will begin to match God's design.

Spirit

Ask God to give you a love for his Word and for strength to obey it. Then tell him thanks for promising to finish his design in you!

Mind Guard

PSALM 119:9

How can a young person
live a pure life?
He can do it by obeying
your word.

I have more understanding than
the elders
because I follow your orders.
I have avoided every evil way
so I could obey your word.
I haven't stopped obeying your laws
because you yourself are my
teacher.
Your promises are so sweet to me.
They are like honey to my mouth!
Your orders give me understanding.
So I hate lying ways.

Your word is like a lamp for my feet
and a light for my way.

PSALM 119:100-105

Psalms

Light on Your Feet

Sword of the Spirit

A good soldier is ready for any situation. Often he travels in the darkest hours of night to avoid being seen by the enemy. But the darkness makes travel hard. He has to have some help to see. Special night-vision goggles or the light of the moon may be all he has to show him the way. God's Word is a lot like the soldier's night-vision goggles.

Our world is so filled with the darkness of sin it is hard to know what is right and wrong. Not even night-vision goggles will help us. But God's Word will shine the light we need to see the truth. When we read and obey the Bible, we find the path to what is right.

Spirit

God's light helps us avoid the traps our enemy sets out for us. It keeps us safe. And it helps us fight the sin inside us.

How well do you know God's Word? Ask God to open your eyes to his truth. Then study his Word every day so you will have the light you need for life!

Mind Guard

PSALM 119:105

Your word is like a lamp
for my feet and a light
for my way.

Wisdom begins with respect for the Lord.

And understanding begins with knowing God, the Holy One.

If you live wisely, you will live a long time.

Wisdom will add years to your life.

The wise person is rewarded by his wisdom.

But a person who makes fun of wisdom will suffer for it.

PROVERBS 9:10-12

Proverbs

Soldier Smarts:
Wearing the Belt of Wisdom

Did you know that some grown-ups are very smart, but they are not wise? In fact, they may be scientists. Doctors. Teachers. It doesn't matter. If they don't know God, they aren't wise.

What is wisdom? It begins with knowing who God is. As we begin to understand that God controls all things, we see that he is in charge and we aren't.

We learn to listen to what he has to say and agree to obey him. We let God teach us through his Word, our parents and our teachers. The more we know and obey what God tells us, the wiser we become. Ask God right now for his help in understanding and obeying him.

Truth

Ask your parents to help you make a card for your teacher at church or school. Draw them a picture of a strong soldier (or whatever you draw best). Thank them for helping you become wise. Remember to thank your parents for teaching you, too!

There is a right time for everything.
Everything on earth has its special
season.
There is a time to be born
and a time to die.
There is a time to plant
and a time to pull up plants.
There is a time to kill
and a time to heal.
There is a time to destroy
and a time to build.
There is a time to cry
and a time to laugh.
There is a time to be sad
and a time to dance.

ECCLESIASTES 3:1-4

Ecclesiastes

Time to Leave

What's your favorite time of year? Do you like the snow in winter? The budding trees and flowers of spring? The hot, hazy days of summer? The cool, crisp air of fall?

Isn't God's world amazing? It is always changing. Every year seasons come and go. The birds and trees and skies know the pattern. They change in perfect rhythm with the time.

God has order for our days, too. He has a perfect time for us to spend learning his Word. We are in training for his good works. When the time is right, he will help us to do the job he has created us to do. He will make us bear fruit. And when we are tired from the journey, he will give us rest. Every time of our lives is a good time to celebrate God's goodness to us.

Treasure Tip

Time itself is a gift from God. How do you spend most of your time each day? Do your activities show a love for God or for yourself? Ask God to help you make the most of every day. Ask him to give you the wisdom and ability to do what he wants you to do every day.

Leave It to God

Go outside in your yard and pick out your favorite tree. Take a leaf from the tree and glue it to a piece of white paper. Label the leaf and the season when you picked it. Then put it in your notebook. Each season, repeat the same steps. At the end of the year, you will see the different ways your tree looks in each season.

SUPPLIES:
tree
rake
leaves
notebook

Tougher Challenge

In the fall, the leaves will turn many beautiful colors. Pick a Saturday to help your parents rake up all the leaves in your yard. Try to create one huge pile. Then celebrate God's goodness by running and jumping into the pile of leaves. When you're done, you can rake them all together again.

There is a time to throw away stones
  and a time to gather them.
There is a time to hug
  and a time not to hug.
There is a time to look for something
  and a time to stop looking for it.
There is a time to keep things
  and a time to throw things away.
There is a time to tear apart
  and a time to sew together.
There is a time to be silent
  and a time to speak.
There is a time to love
  and a time to hate.
There is a time for war
  and a time for peace.

ECCLESIASTES 3:5-8

It's About Time

Guard Your Heart

You've been playing with the building blocks making a giant fort. Suddenly the teacher says it's time to put up the toys and sit down for the lesson. You:

★ **A** Pretend that you didn't hear her and keep building.

★ **B** Start arguing that you aren't finished with your fort.

★ **C** Put the building blocks away and find your seat.

★ **D** Smash the fort to show how angry you are.

God says that he gives us the time we need to do what he wants. When it is time to play, you should play with all your energy. But when the time comes for learning, it is time to put the toys aside. There is a time for talking, and a time for being quiet. A time to be silly, and a time to be serious.

Heart

Ask God to help you have an obedient heart to do what he wants you to do, when he wants you to do it. Then make the most of your time. Trust him to take you on many adventures as you learn to follow him through all the different times of your life!

Two people are better than one.
They get more done by working
together.
If one person falls,
the other can help him up.
But it is bad for the person who is alone
when he falls.
No one is there to help him.
If two lie down together, they will be
warm.
But a person alone will not be warm.
An enemy might defeat one person,
but two people together can defend
themselves.

ECCLESIASTES 4:9-12

Ecclesiastes

Reinforcements

Your commanding officer has just given you orders. You are to take the enemy down as quickly as you can. The foe is smart and well-armed. Your mission is dangerous.

Would you be scared? Would you go it alone, or would you enlist help from other soldiers?

If you're smart, you'd ask for help. God says that he wants his soldiers to work together in the fight against sin and Satan. We aren't ever supposed to go it alone.

So what should you do to carry out God's fighting orders? Find friends around you who love God, too. Look for kids at school, at church and in your neighborhood who want to know Jesus better.

Faith

Talk to your parents. Even your teachers at school can help you be strong if they belong to Jesus. Like a band of brothers, God's people will encourage you and help you outsmart the enemy. Together we can win the war that Satan wages against us.

The Lord says:
"These people say they love me,
    They show honor to me with words.
    But their hearts are far from me.
The honor they show me
    is nothing but human rules they
        have memorized.
So I will continue to amaze these people
    by doing more and more miracles.
Their wise men will lose their wisdom.
    Their wise men will not be able to
        understand."

How terrible it will be for those who try
    to hide things from the Lord.
How terrible it will be for those who
    do their work in darkness.
    They think no one will see them or
        know what they do.

You are confused.
      You think the clay is equal to the potter.
You think that an object can tell the
            person who made it,
      "You didn't make me."
This is like a pot telling its maker,
      "You don't know anything."

In a very short time, Lebanon will
            become rich farmland.
      And the rich farmland will seem
            like a forest.
At that time the deaf will hear the
            words in a book.
      Instead of having darkness and
            gloom, the blind will see.
The Lord will make the poor people happy.
      They will rejoice in the Holy One
            of Israel.

ISAIAH 29:13-19

Do What You Say

Stand Strong

What would you do if you had a friend who never played with you? Even if they said they liked you, you might not believe them. If they were your friend and liked you, they should spend time with you.

Jesus says that he feels the same way. It's easy to say we love God. We may even tell other people about him. But do we show it by the way we act? Do we really take time to talk to Jesus and obey what he says in the Bible?

When we tell others about Jesus, it is important to tell them the truth. But it is also important for them to see that we believe the truth. They will be watching our lives to see if we obey what we believe to be true. Real faith always brings real fruit. Ask Jesus today to help your actions to match your words.

Strong

The Lord wants to show his mercy
to you.
He wants to rise and comfort you.
The Lord is a fair God.
And everyone who waits for his
help will be happy.

You people who live on Mount Zion in Jerusalem will not cry anymore. The Lord will hear your crying, and he will comfort you. The Lord will hear you, and he will help you. The Lord has given you sorrow and hurt. It was like the bread and water you ate every day. But he is your teacher, and he will not continue to hide from you. You will see your teacher with your own eyes. If you go the wrong way—to the right or to the left—you will hear a voice behind you. It will say, "This is the right way. You should go this way."

ISAIAH 30:18-21

On Course

Sword of the Spirit

When your mom wants you to do something, how do you know what she wants? She tells you, of course! It's up to you to listen and obey.

Did you know that God speaks to you, too? His voice is often hard to hear. We have to listen with our spiritual ears. If we want to hear him, we have to be still and quiet. We have to wait patiently for God's perfect time.

God says that he will lead us the right way at the right time. He will use the Bible verses you have already learned to help you know the way. He may use the verses you are reading now with your parents. When God brings his Word to your mind, he is speaking to you. Listen!

Spirit

hen ask God for strength to obey what you know is right. Thank him for caring about you. Praise God for his Word that leads us where we need to go!

Memory Portion

Mind Guard

ISAIAH 30:21

If you go the wrong way—to the right or to the left—you will hear a voice behind you. It will say, "This is the right way. You should go this way."

You people say,
"Come, let's go back to the Lord.
He has hurt us, but he will heal us.
    He has wounded us, but he will
        bandage our wounds.
In a short while he will put new life
        in us.
    We will not have to wait long for
        him to raise us up.
    Then we may live in his presence.
Let's learn about the Lord.
    Let's try hard to know who he is.
He will come to us
    as surely as the dawn comes.
The Lord will come to us like the rain,
    like the spring rain that waters the
        ground."

The Lord says, "Israel, what should
    I do with you?
    Judah, what should I do with you?
Your faithfulness is like a morning
    mist.
    It lasts only as long as the dew in
    the morning.
I have warned you by my prophets
    that I will kill you and destroy you.
    My judgments will flash forth like
    lightning against you.
I want faithful love
    more than I want animal sacrifices.
I want people to know me
    more than I want burnt offerings."

Hosea

HOSEA 6:1-6

By Dawn's Early Light

Helmet of Salvation

It's almost like magic. If you wake up early enough in the morning and walk out on the grass, you feel the wetness under your feet. Every morning the dew forms on the grass and leaves. But by noon, the sun has dried it up.

In Hosea, God uses the picture of dew to warn his people. They loved God at first. They used to obey him. But as they got older, they forgot his ways.

Like dew on the grass, their love for God vanished.

God said he was tired of them saying they believed in him when their lives didn't show it. He wanted them to prove their love by obeying God's Word.

We need our love for God to stay strong all day, every day. Ask God to help you discover who he really is. Pray that he will help you love him all of the time.

Salvation

You are the salt of the earth. But if the salt loses it salty taste, it cannot be made salty again. It is good for nothing. It must be thrown out for people to walk on.

You are the light that gives light to the world. A city that is built on a hill cannot be hidden. And people don't hide a light under a bowl. They put the light on a lampstand. Then the light shines for all the people in the house. In the same way you should be a light for other people. Live so that they will see the good things you do. Live so that they will praise your Father in heaven.

MATTHEW 5:13-16

Always a Soldier

Stand Strong

You are in the store with your mom when you spy the coolest toy you've ever seen. You feel like you've just got to have it, so you ask your mom for it. Not surprised she said no, you ask again. Then again. Then you decide to add your whiny voice and start to beg. Soon, you know you'll be in a full temper tantrum.

Stop for a moment. Did God say you can go off duty as his soldier whenever you feel like it? No, God says that we are his salt and light. We are to show his love so well that, like salt, it actually makes others around us thirsty for God. We are to speak truth so others will come to the light. We must behave like God's soldiers and children at all places and at all times.

Strong

We must fight the sin in our hearts and choose what is right. It honors God, and it helps the people around us who don't know Jesus to see the truth in action. When you are tempted to sin, ask God for strength to let his light shine through you.

You have heard that it was said to our people long ago, "When you make a promise, don't break your promise. Keep the promises that you make to the Lord." But I tell you, never make an oath. Don't make an oath using the name of heaven, because heaven is God's throne. Don't make an oath using the name of the earth, because the earth belongs to God. Don't make an oath using the name of Jerusalem, because that is the city of the great King. And don't even say that your own head is proof that you will keep your oath. You cannot make one hair on your head become white or black. Say only "yes" if you mean "yes," and say only "no" if you mean "no." If you must say more than "yes" or "no," it is from the Evil One.

MATTHEW 5:33-37

On My Honor

You promised your sister that you would let her have your sword if she let you have her candy. However, now that you've eaten the candy, you decide to:

A Let her keep the sword since you promised.

B Grab the sword back from her when she isn't expecting it.

C Tell her you were just joking and you want your sword back now.

139

Jesus wants us to tell the truth. He wants us to be so truthful that we don't even need to make promises. Whenever we simply say we are going to do something, we need to do it.

The next time you start to make a promise, take a moment to think about it. Do you really mean what you are about to say?

Heart

Are you really able to make it happen? If not, you need to keep your mouth shut. Ask God to give you the wisdom you need to speak only truth without making hasty promises.

When you pray, don't be like the hypocrites. They love to stand in the synagogues and on the street corners and pray loudly. They want people to see them pray. I tell you the truth. They already have their full reward. When you pray, you should go into your room and close the door. Then pray to your Father who cannot be seen. Your Father can see what is done in secret, and he will reward you.

And when you pray, don't be like those people who don't know God. They continue saying things that mean nothing. They think that God will hear them because of the many things they say. Don't be like them. Your Father knows the things you need before you ask him.

MATTHEW 6:5-8

Super Powers

Would you want to be a superhero with super powers? If you belong to Jesus, you are one! In fact, God says you have all the power you need to live a holy and good life through his Spirit.

He even gives you a secret weapon for the fight: prayer! Prayer is our direct connection with God. By talking out loud or in our minds to God, we can ask for help in every situation.

It's good to pray in the morning when you wake up, before meals and at night. But don't stop there! God wants us to stay in touch with him all the time. Are you feeling tempted to sin? Pray for help. Are you confused about what is right or wrong? Ask God for wisdom. Do you need strength for the day? God will give it if you ask.

Faith

We need God in every moment we live. Remember that prayer is your secret weapon to win the victory over evil every day.

I tell you, don't worry about the food you need to live. And don't worry about the clothes you need for your body. Life is more important than food. And the body is more important than clothes. Look at the birds in the air. They don't plant or harvest or store food in barns. But your heavenly Father feeds the birds. And you know that you are worth much more than the birds. You cannot add any time to your life by worrying about it.

And why do you worry about clothes? Look at the flowers in the field. See how they grow. They don't work or make clothes for themselves. But I tell you that even Solomon with his riches was not dressed as beautifully as one of these flowers. God clothes the grass in the field like that. The grass is living today, but tomorrow it is thrown into the fire to be burned. So you can be even more sure that God will clothe you. Don't have so little faith! Don't worry and say, "What will we eat?" or "What will we drink?" or "What will we wear?" All the people who don't know God keep trying to get these things. And your Father in heaven knows that you need them. The thing you should want most is God's kingdom and doing what God wants. Then all these other things you need will be given to you.

MATTHEW 6:25-33

Fear Factor

Sword of the Spirit

Not every soldier is always brave. In fact, each one may be afraid of something different. After all, war is scary. You don't know what will happen next.

God knows that all his soldiers worry. He knows we get afraid of many different things. What worries you? What do you do when you get scared?

God says we don't need to worry. He is in control of everything that happens in our lives. He is taking care of us! He gives us everything we need to live and fight well.

We just need to keep our eyes on him. We must remember his promise to provide for us all our lives.

Whenever you get scared, talk to Jesus. Tell him what's on your mind. Ask him to take care of it. Ask him for his peace. He'll give it to you! He'll change your fear into stronger faith in him.

Memory Portion

Mind Guard

MATTHEW 6:33

The thing you should want most is God's kingdom and doing what God wants. Then all these other things you need will be given to you.

The kingdom of heaven is like a treasure hidden in a field. One day a man found the treasure, and then he hid it in the field again. The man was very happy to find the treasure. He went and sold everything that he owned to buy that field.

Also, the kingdom of heaven is like a man looking for fine pearls. One day he found a very valuable pearl. The man went and sold everything he had to buy that pearl.

MATTHEW 13:44-45

Matthew

Dig This

Jesus said that the kingdom of heaven is like a treasure hidden in a field. In Jesus' parable, he told how a man discovered the treasure. So what did he do? He buried it again!

Then he went to the man who owned the field and bought the whole field from him.

Treasure Tip

Jesus continued the story by saying that looking for heaven is similar to looking for fine pearls. When the man found one, he sold everything he had to buy it. God wants us to love him and his kingdom more than anything else on this earth. There is no greater treasure than a personal relationship with Jesus! We need to spend our time and energy seeking after him.

Quest

The Dirt on Pearls

SUPPLIES:
1 strand of costume jewelry
(like Mardi Gras beads
or plastic pearls found
at a dollar store)
1 bucket of dirt

Find a good place outside for your bucket of dirt. Then add water to the dirt to make a nice batch of mud. Have a parent or sibling break apart the beads from the necklace and hide them in the mud. Ask them to spread the beads throughout the bucket. Also, have them count the number of beads they put into the mud.

Use a stopwatch to time yourself. Dig through the mud to find the pearls. Were you able to find all the treasure? How long did it take you to find all the beads? Was it easy or hard work? When you're finished, hide the treasure again. Then invite your brothers or sisters to give it a try!

A Canaanite woman from that area came to Jesus. The woman cried out, "Lord, Son of David, please help me! My daughter has a demon, and she is suffering very much."

... Jesus answered, "God sent me only to the lost sheep, the people of Israel."

Then the woman came to Jesus again. She bowed before him and said, "Lord, help me!"

Jesus answered, "It is not right to take the children's bread and give it to the dogs."

The woman said, "Yes, Lord, but even the dogs eat the pieces of food that fall from their masters' table."

Then Jesus answered, "Woman, you have great faith! I will do what you asked me to do." And at that moment the woman's daughter was healed.

MATTHEW 15:22, 24-28

Perfect Permission

Guard Your Heart

You are in the middle of your favorite video game when your dad tells you it's time to get ready for bed. You decide to:

A Ignore him until he has asked at least two more times.

B Tell him you're coming, but keep on playing until you finish the game.

C Get up and complain about how your game was ruined.

D Hit the pause button and ask your dad if you can finish the game before bedtime.

Your parents are in charge of you. But they don't want to make your life bad. In fact, they love you and want the very best for you.

Just like the woman in Matthew 15, you need to ask for permission with respect if there is something you need. That means asking with the right heart attitude and the right tone of voice. Then they will listen to your request.

Heart

God gives them the wisdom they need to know if the answer should be "yes" or "no." When they answer you, obey with a happy heart.

Your thoughtful words and obedient actions help your friendship with your parents and God grow stronger.

Jesus went to the area of Caesarea Philippi. He said to his followers, "I am the Son of Man. Who do the people say I am?"

They answered, "Some people say you are John the Baptist. Others say you are Elijah. And others say that you are Jeremiah or one of the prophets."

Then Jesus asked them, "And who do you say I am?"

Simon Peter answered, "You are the Christ, the Son of the living God."

Jesus answered, "You are blessed, Simon son of Jonah. No person taught you that. My Father in heaven showed you who I am. So I tell you, you are Peter. And I will build my church on this rock. The power of death will not be able to defeat my church. I will give you the keys of the kingdom of heaven. The things you don't allow on earth will be the things that God does not allow. The things you allow on earth will be the things that God allows." Then Jesus warned his followers not to tell anyone that he was the Christ.

MATTHEW 16:13-20

Matthew

Fisher of Men: Peter

The Bible talks a lot about Peter in the Gospels. He was one of the men counted as Jesus' closest friends. So what made him so special?

God did. Really, Peter was just a regular fisherman when he first met Jesus. What makes him stand out from the rest was that he believed Jesus was telling the truth. He trusted Jesus with his life and left his fishing nets behind. He followed Jesus everywhere he went and learned much about God as he did.

Peter was not perfect at all. He talked too much. He often didn't understand Jesus' plan. But God was patient with Peter. Jesus corrected his wrong thinking. And God opened Peter's eyes to see that Jesus was God's one and only Son.

God used Peter to spread the truth about Jesus all over the world. God can use you, too. You simply need to believe that Jesus is Lord. Then give him your life like Peter did. God will make you a great fisher of men, too!

Warriors

No one knows when that day or time will be. Even the Son and the angels in heaven don't know. Only the Father knows. When the Son of Man comes, it will be the same as what happened during Noah's time. In those days before the flood, people were eating and drinking. They were marrying and giving their children to be married. They were still doing those things until the day Noah entered the boat. They knew nothing about what was happening. But then the flood came, and all those people were destroyed.

It will be the same when the Son of Man comes. Two men will be working together in the field. One man will be taken and the other left. Two women will be grinding grain with a hand mill. One woman will be taken and the other will be left.

So always be ready. You don't know the day your Lord will come.

MATTHEW 24:36-42

Matthew

Eyes to the Skies

Shield of Faith

The battle has been hard. How long will the fight go on? Take heart! The story ends well. In the end, the hero returns and destroys the enemy for good. The people are saved and live happily ever after.

Want to know what's so great about fairy tales? They show us what is really true. We do have a Hero. Jesus has promised to come back to earth one day. When he comes for the second time, no one will wonder if he is God. Everyone will see and know.

Jesus will destroy Satan and his demons. Death and sin will also be defeated. Jesus will win, and God's people will celebrate the victory. We will live happily with him forever!

Do you get tired of fighting sin? Don't give up. Our Hero will come again some day. He promises to take us to heaven. Ask him for strength to keep fighting as a good warrior for him here on earth. But keep your eyes on the skies looking for his return!

Faith

Then the king will say to the good people on his right, "Come My Father has given you his blessing. Come and receive the kingdom God has prepared for you since the world was made. I was hungry, and you gave me food. I was thirsty, and you gave me something to drink. I was alone and away from home, and you invited me into your house. I was without clothes, and you gave me something to wear. I was sick, and you cared for me. I was in prison, and you visited me."

Then the good people will answer, "Lord, when did we see you hungry and give you food? When did we see you thirsty and give you something to drink? When did we see you alone and away from home and invite you into our house? When did we see you without clothes and give you something to wear? When did we see you sick or in prison and care for you?"

Then the King will answer, "I tell you the truth. Anything you did for any of my people here, you also did for me."

MATTHEW 25:34-40

Matthew

Out of Formation

"**H**oney, would you like to have someone over today?" your mom asks. Quickly you start thinking through your list of closest friends. But your mom adds one catch. "Why don't you ask someone new that you don't know very well?"

We are always comfortable and happy with our friends. We feel safe and strong when we know what to expect. But God wants us to trust him a little more. We have to get out of our usual "formation" to experience new adventures he has for us.

He may have other kids in your class at school or church who need your friendship. He may have planned for you to learn something new from them, too.

God wants us to keep watch over the people he has placed in our lives. Ask God if anyone you know is hurting or in need of a friend. Then ask him for the strength and courage it takes to reach out to them and the wisdom to know how to do that. It's your chance to serve God, help another, and grow stronger in your faith!

Strong

Joseph and Mary finished doing everything that the law of the Lord commanded. Then they went home to Nazareth, their own town in Galilee. The little child began to grow up. He became stronger and wiser, and God's blessings were with him.

LUKE 2:39-40

Luke

Growing Strong

Sword of the Spirit

You aren't the only one. Jesus had to grow up, too. At one point, Jesus was even your age!

The Bible doesn't tell us much about Jesus' childhood. It does say that he was raised in a godly home. And Jesus grew up, becoming taller and wiser every day until the time was right for his ministry to begin.

You are busy growing up, too. You learn new things almost every day. But as you are growing bigger and stronger, God wants you to remember him. You need to grow your mind, too. You need to understand God and know his Word better and better every day. How can you do that?

Spirit

You need to pray for wisdom!
You also need to look for God in the
Bible. Memorize the truth you find there.
Over time, you will become stronger and
wiser, just like Jesus did.

Mind Guard

LUKE 2:40

The little child began to grow up.
He became stronger and wiser,
and God's blessings were
with him.

Jesus . . . went to Capernaum. In Capernaum there was an army officer. He had a servant who was so sick he was nearly dead. The officer loved the servant very much. When the officer heard about Jesus, he sent some Jewish elders to him. The officer wanted the leaders to ask Jesus to come and heal his servant. The men went to Jesus and begged him saying, "This officer is worthy of your help. He loves our people, and he built us a synagogue."

LUKE 7:1-5

Luke

Faith of Champions: The Army Officer

Want to know what big faith looks like? Look no further than the army officer in Luke 7. Even Jesus was impressed with just how much this man believed God.

The officer had a sick servant. He wanted Jesus to heal him. But when Jesus started to head toward his house, the officer had Jesus stopped.

He told Jesus through his servant that he had no need for Jesus to come. He knew that Jesus had authority just like he did. In fact, Jesus had even more power because he could heal sickness. Jesus marveled over his faith.

Jesus did heal the army officer's servant. He also praised the officer for understanding Jesus' position of authority. The officer shows us what it means to believe Jesus.

Warriors

Do you believe Jesus is the Son of God? Do you know that he is in charge of your life, too? If you have trouble believing, ask Jesus for help with your faith. Then trust that God will grow your faith, just like he did for the army officer.

Jesus said, "A man was going down the road from Jerusalem to Jericho. Some robbers attacked him. They tore off his clothes and beat him. Then they left him lying there, almost dead. It happened that a Jewish priest was going down that road. When the priest saw the man, he walked by on the other side of the road. Next, a Levite came there. He went over and looked at the man. Then he walked by on the other side of the road. Then a Samaritan traveling down the road came to where the hurt man was lying. He saw the man and felt very sorry for him. The Samaritan went to him and poured olive oil and wine on his wounds and bandaged them. He put the hurt man on his own donkey and took him to an inn. At the inn, the Samaritan took care of him. The next day, the Samaritan brought out two silver coins and gave them to the innkeeper. The Samaritan said, 'Take care of this man. If you spend more money on him, I will pay it back to you when I come again.'"

Then Jesus said, "Which one of these three men do you think was a neighbor to the man who was attacked by the robbers?"

The teacher of the law answered, "The one who helped him."

Jesus said to him, "Then go and do the same thing he did!"

LUKE 10:30-37

Care for Action?:
Wearing the Belt of Caring

What happens when you fall down and scrape your knee? Sometimes you can get up and keep playing. But other times it really hurts. You need help from someone who cares.

Did you know that God wants you to be caring, too? You need to be on the lookout for people who need help. Maybe they have fallen down and need a helping hand.

Maybe their hearts are hurting because they are lonely or sad. Maybe they need a friend. Don't look the other way when you see a need. Be bold and brave. Ask how you can help. Then be joyful! God says that when we help others, we are actually serving him.

ACTIVITY

Make it your mission today to take care of others. Put a bandage on the back of each hand to remind you what to do. Then watch for the people God will put in your life who need your help. Thank God each time you have a chance to serve him by helping others!

Suppose a woman has ten silver coins, but she loses one of them. She will light a lamp and clean the house. She will look carefully for the coin until she finds it. And when she finds it, she will call her friends and neighbors and say, "Be happy with me because I have found the coin that I lost!" In the same way, there is joy before the angels of God when 1 sinner changes his heart.

LUKE 15:8-10

Luke

Coin Caper

Jesus had a strange story to tell. A woman had ten coins, but she lost one. So what's the big deal? She still had nine others, right? She still had nine coins, but every coin was very valuable to her.

She searched high and low all over her house to find the missing coin. Her pain and perseverance finally paid off!

Treasure Tip

Jesus' story meant more than a treasure hunt for coins. Jesus was describing how God feels when one sinner repents of his sins. God and all the angels in heaven rejoice when we turn from sin and become a part of God's family. Once we were lost . . . but now we are found!

Quest

ACTIVITY

Lost and Found

How do you think the woman felt as she searched for her lost coin? Find out for yourself: Have a parent or sibling hide a quarter somewhere in the living room. Use a stopwatch to time yourself. How long did it take you to find the coin? What was your reaction when you found it?

Tougher Challenge

Try the same game again, only this time, turn out the lights. Just like the woman who used a lamp to light her way, use a flashlight to guide you around the room. Is it harder to find the treasure in the dark? How is the flashlight helpful in the search?

Jesus was going through the city of Jericho. In Jericho there was a man named Zacchaeus. He was a wealthy, very important tax collector. He wanted to see who Jesus was, but he was too short to see above the crowd. He ran ahead to a place where he knew Jesus would come. He climbed a sycamore tree so he could see Jesus. When Jesus came to that place, he looked up and saw Zacchaeus in the tree. He said to him, "Zacchaeus, hurry and come down! I must stay at your house today."

Zacchaeus came down quickly. He was pleased to have Jesus in his house.

LUKE 19:1-6

Luke

Get a Good Altitude

What else was a short man to do? Zacchaeus wanted to see Jesus. The problem was the crowd of people that always followed him. How could he ever see above their heads to catch a glimpse of the Savior?

You know the story. Zacchaeus climbed a tree. At last he could see Jesus.

And guess what he discovered? Jesus had already seen him! In fact, Jesus wanted to visit him at his own house. Zacchaeus's life would never be the same. He invited Jesus into his life and repented of his sins. He gave back money he had stolen from others. He lived a new life in Jesus from that day forward.

Treasure Tip

Sometimes it's hard to feel important when you are young and small. But you are! God sees you clearly, and he wants to be a part of your life, too. God sees our lives very differently than we do. He knows what is really important. And he wants to help us see life the way he sees it. Ask God to help you see yourself and others the way he does. Ask him to be a part of your life, just like Zacchaeus did!

ACTIVITY

Tree Climbing

Take a visit to a local park or around your neighborhood where you know you might find some good climbing trees. If you can't find any, you could use a stepladder in your backyard, or try climbing up onto your mom or dad's shoulders. Imagine yourself as Zacchaeus, climbing above the crowds. What would you see? How does the world look different when you're higher up?

SUPPLIES:
a good pair of tennis shoes

a parent (or other adult) for supervision

Jesus said, "My food is to do what the One who sent me wants me to do. My food is to finish the work that he gave me to do. You say, 'Four more months to wait before we gather the grain.' But I tell you, open your eyes. Look at the fields that are ready for harvesting now. Even now, the one who harvests the crop is being paid. He is gathering crops for eternal life. So now the one who plants can be happy along with the one who harvests. It is true when we say, 'One person plants, but another harvests the crop.' I sent you to harvest a crop that you did not work for. Others did the work, and you get the profit from their work."

JOHN 4:34-38

John

Field Operation

Stand Strong

Have you ever seen a cotton field that is ready to be picked? The whole land looks like snow because the white fluffy balls of cotton pop out of their brown seed pods.

God says the world around us is like a giant field ready to be picked. He has people all over the place who are ready to become Christians. They just need us to go to them and tell them about Jesus.

You don't have to know everything about God to share your faith. Just tell others the Good News you know. We need to repent of our sins and believe that Jesus will forgive us and give us a new life. We get to be friends with God and have a place in heaven, just by trusting Jesus to save us.

Strong

Take time today to thank God for his Good News. Ask him for the chance to share it with someone else, too!

Jesus answered, "Are you looking for me because you saw me do miracles? No! I tell you the truth. You are looking for me because you ate the bread and were satisfied. Earthly food spoils and ruins. So don't work to get that kind of food. But work to get the food that stays good always and gives you eternal life. The Son of Man will give you that food. God the Father has shown that he is with the Son of Man."

The people asked Jesus, "What are the things God wants us to do?"

Jesus answered, "The work God wants you to do is this: to believe in the One that God sent."

JOHN 6:26-29

John

Official Duty

Shield of Faith

Adam and Eve broke their friendship with God because they believed Satan instead of God. So God had to fix what Adam and Eve had broken.

God has made a way for all of us to have a close friendship with him. He gives us forgiveness through Jesus. We must trust that Jesus' death on the cross is enough to pay for our sins.

We have to trust that God will be true to his promise to save us, even though we don't deserve it.

Satan would like us to think that we can get to heaven by doing good. But he's lying again. We need to quit listening to lies and start listening to God. If God says he loves us and forgives us because of Jesus, our job is to believe him.

Faith

Do you have trouble trusting God instead of your own ideas? Ask God to help your unbelief. Ask him to build your faith so you can fight against the enemy's lies.

A man named Ananias and his wife Sapphira sold some land. But he gave only part of the money to the apostles. He secretly kept some of it for himself. His wife knew about this, and she agreed to it. Peter said, "Ananias, why did you let Satan rule your heart? You lied to the Holy Spirit. Why did you keep part of the money you received for the land for yourself? Before you sold the land, it belonged to you. And even after you sold it, you could have used the money any way you wanted. Why did you think of doing this? You lied to God, not to men!" When Ananias heard this, he fell down and died. Some young men came in, wrapped up his body, carried it out, and buried it. And everyone who heard about this was filled with fear.

ACTS 5:1-6

So Help Me God:
Wearing the Belt of Truth

Ananias and Sapphira had given the apostles money. So why did God kill them?

Ananias and Sapphira lied to God and the apostles. They pretended like they were giving all their money away. But they tried to secretly keep some for themselves.

We can't keep any secrets from God.

He knows what we are thinking, doing and saying all the time. He says that he wants us to always tell the truth.

Sometimes it is hard to be completely honest. Even though it may be scary, God says he will give you the strength to always do what is right. Ask God to help you always tell the truth.

Truth

ACTIVITY

We need to fight the enemy by always being honest. Ask your parents to help you find a thin strip of leather or brightly colored yarn. Tie it around your waist or wrist to remind you of the belt of truth. Ask Jesus to help you speak the truth, no matter what.

Stephen was richly blessed by God. God gave him the power to do great miracles and signs among the people. But some Jews were against him. They belonged to a synagogue of Free Men (as it was called). (This synagogue was also for Jews from Cyrene and from Alexandria.) Jews from Cilicia and Asia were also with them. They all came and argued with Stephen.

But the Spirit was helping him to speak with wisdom. His words were so strong that they could not argue with him. So they paid some men to say, "We heard him say things against Moses and against God!"

This upset the people, the Jewish elders, and the teachers of the law. They came to Stephen, grabbed him and brought him to a meeting of the Jewish leaders.... All the people in the meeting were watching Stephen closely. His face looked like the face of an angel.

ACTS 6:8-12, 15

Acts

Strength in Action: Stephen

Mighty Warriors

Stephen was a very strong man, but not because of his muscles. The Bible says that Stephen had very strong faith that gave him the power to do God's mighty work.

God filled Stephen with his Holy Spirit. God gave him the power to do many miracles and signs, just like Jesus did. When Stephen preached the Word of God, the Holy Spirit worked in powerful ways to change people's hearts.

God used Stephen to help lead many others to faith in Christ.

Stephen trusted Jesus so much that he became the first man to be killed for his faith. As he was dying, Stephen saw heaven opened, with Jesus standing there waiting to welcome him home.

Can you be brave and strong like Stephen? You can't do it on your own. But if God fills you with his Spirit, you can lead a powerful life of faith, too. Ask Jesus right now to fill you with his Spirit and the faith you need to follow him wherever he leads.

Warriors

In the church at Antioch there were these prophets and teachers: Barnabas, Simeon (also called Niger), Lucius (from the city of Cyrene), Manaen (who had grown up with Herod, the ruler) and Saul. They were all worshiping the Lord and giving up eating. The Holy Spirit said to them, "Give Barnabas and Saul to me to do a special work. I have chosen them for it."

So they gave up eating and prayed. They laid their hands on Barnabas and Saul and sent them out.

Barnabas and Saul were sent out by the Holy Sprit. They went to the city of Seleucia. From there they sailed to the island of Cyprus.

ACTS 13:1-4

Change in Heart: Paul

Mighty Warriors

D... one is beyond ... Do ... know someone who s...on't give up. Ask God ... change that person's heart. ... help them see Jesus, just

will never c'...

Nothing ...

God. Jus...

name w:...

hated C...

job to ...

believ ...

them ...

into p...

killed ...

Chris...

I must serve all people—Greeks and non-Greeks, the wise and the foolish. That is why I want so much to preach the Good News to you in Rome.

I am not ashamed of the Good News. It is the power God uses to save everyone who believes—to save the Jews first, and then to save the non-Jews.

ROMANS 1:14-16

Romans

Scared to Talk?

Almost every soldier will say it. They get scared in battle. They don't know what the enemy might do next. And they know that they can get hurt.

As God's soldiers, we get scared, too. We know we need to tell other people about Jesus. We need to let them know about God's forgiveness through Jesus.

Stand Strong

But often we are afraid to speak. We don't know what they will say back to us. We are afraid that they might not believe us. They might even make fun of us.

When God gives you a chance to share the Good News with others, ask him to help you to be brave. Your words can help set your friend free from the enemy! Don't be embarrassed. God says his Word is very powerful.

Strong

It can change even the hardest heart. Trust God to do his work in others as you speak his truth. Then trust God to turn their hearts to him in his time.

Brothers, since God has shown us great mercy, I beg you to offer your lives as a living sacrifice to him. Your offering must be only for God and pleasing to him. This is the spiritual way for you to worship. Do not be shaped by this world. Instead be changed within by a new way of thinking. Then you will be able to decide what God wants for you. And you will be able to know what is good and pleasing to God and what is perfect.

ROMANS 12:1-2

Romans

Mind Field

Sword of the Spirit

You might hate it…or you might really like it.

Either way, you must take a bath whenever you get really dirty. You were meant to be clean! Admit it. After it's over, it feels pretty good to get the grime off.

Our minds are a lot like our bodies. Our minds get dirty when we start to believe Satan's lies. Every time we listen to what the world says is true instead of what God says, our minds get a little dirtier.

So God says we need to get clean! He says that we need to make our minds fresh and new again by remembering the truth found in God's Word.

Can you think of something you have said or thought today that wasn't true (like "Nobody likes me." or "It's okay as long as I don't get caught.")?

Spirit

What does God have to say about it? Ask Jesus to help you notice whenever you are believing a lie. Then confess it to him, and renew your mind with the truth.

Mind Guard

ROMANS 12:2

Do not be shaped by this world. Instead be changed within by a new way of thinking. Then you will be able to decide what God wants for you. And you will be able to know what is good and pleasing to God and what is perfect.

If someone does wrong to you, do not pay him back by doing wrong to him. Try to do what everyone thinks is right. Do your best to live in peace with everyone. My friends, do not try to punish others when they wrong you. Wait for God to punish them with his anger. It is written: "I am the One who punishes; I will pay people back," says the Lord. But you should do this:

"If your enemy is hungry, feed him;
    if your enemy is thirsty, give him
    a drink.
Doing this will be like pouring
    burning coals on his head."

Proverbs 25:21-22

Do not let evil defeat you. Defeat evil by doing good.

ROMANS 12:17-21

A Kind of Counterattack:
Wearing the Belt of Kindness

Your little brother has launched an attack . . . on you. He is teasing you about almost everything. You're ready to give him a good smack on the head.

But wait. God has a better idea. God wants you to get even in a whole new way. He wants you to be just as kind as your brother is mean.

Instead of fighting back, God calls his soldiers to love. When we choose to forgive and love instead of fight, we defeat evil. God gets glory. And we get the joy of better friendships and hearts filled with peace.

Truth

Who do you fight with the most? Think of three ways you can show love to him or her the next time they try to bother you. Then when the moment comes, launch your counterattack! Pour on the love, and watch your Lord come to the rescue!

Is Apollos important? No! Is Paul important? No! We are only servants of God who helped you believe. Each one of us did the work God gave us to do. I planted the seed of the teaching in you, and Apollos watered it. But God is the One who made the seed grow. So the one who plants is not important, and the one who waters is not important. Only God is important, because he is the One who makes things grow. The one who plants and the one who waters have the same purpose. And each will be rewarded for his own work. We are workers together for God. And you are like a farm that belongs to God.

1 CORINTHIANS 3:5-9

1 Corinthians

Insider Secrets

Stand Strong

Have you ever planted a seed? At first, it might look like nothing will happen. The seed just sits buried in the dirt. Over time, with sun and water, you will see a sprout spring up. Then soon, you will see a large plant where the seed once was.

Jesus says that sharing his Word with others is very similar to planting seeds. Each of God's children plays a part in the planting process. If we have a chance to tell someone about Jesus, we need to speak up. We are shining the sun or raining the rain on the seed God has planted in their hearts. In God's time, he will make them grow to understand who Jesus is.

Strong

Don't ever give up on anyone. God is able to make anyone grow a heart that loves him. Thank God for letting you be a part of his incredible plan!

I am not trying to make you feel ashamed. I am writing this to give you a warning as if you were my own dear children. For though you may have 10,000 teachers in Christ, you do not have many fathers. Through the Good News I became your father in Christ Jesus. So I beg you, please be like me. That is why I am sending Timothy to you. He is my son in the Lord. I love Timothy, and he is faithful. He will help you remember the way I live in Christ Jesus. This way of life is what I teach in all the churches everywhere.

1 CORINTHIANS 4:14-17

Trained in Truth: Timothy

Have you ever wondered how your father or another brave man you know got to be so strong?

All men start off as baby boys. Then they grow. If they receive good training from their parents or the Lord, they often grow to become strong men of faith.

Timothy was very young when he became a Christian through his mother and grandmother's teaching.

Then he joined Paul in his ministry work. Paul trained Timothy in the truth. Even though he was much younger than other leaders, God used Timothy. Timothy encouraged the believers in the truth. Paul told Timothy to never worry about his age. God can use people of any age to do his work if they are willing to obey.

Warriors

You are young and in training, just like Timothy. Ask God to help you obey now so you will grow into a strong man of God. Thank him for letting you be a part of his great work when you're young and old!

Remember this: The person who plants a little will have a small harvest. But the person who plants a lot will have a big harvest. Each one should give, then, what he has decided in his heart to give. He should not give if it makes him sad. And he should not give if he thinks he is forced to give. God loves the person who gives happily. And God can give you more blessings than you need. Then you will always have plenty of everything. You will have enough to give to every good work. It is written in the Scriptures:

"He gives freely to the poor.
   The things he does are right and
      will continue forever." *Psalm 112:9*
God is the one who gives seed to the
farmer. And he gives bread for food.
And God will give you all the seed
you need to make it grow. He will
make a great harvest from your
goodness. God will make you rich in
every way so that you can always
give freely. And your giving through
us will cause many to give thanks
to God.

2 CORINTHIANS 9:6-11

2 Corinthians

A Soldier's Sacrifice:
Wearing the Belt of Generosity

Belt of Truth

Your dad just gave you a brand-new set of toy soldiers. Now you have everything you need to make your army complete. You just have one problem. Your little brother wants a couple of your men to play with. What should you do?

You may want to run and hide your toys. You might even put up a fight.

But God says there's a better way. He tells us to give with a cheerful heart.

If we believe God is taking care of us, we can give to others in need. Our generous hearts make God happy. He is able to use even the smallest gifts to build his kingdom. He uses our gifts to help us and others know him better.

ACTIVITY

Look around your room. Ask your parents if you can give any new or unused toys to a local charity or a family in need. Remember to thank God for always meeting your needs.

We do live in the world. But we do not fight in the same way that the world fights. We fight with weapons that are different from those the world uses. Our weapons have power from God. These weapons can destroy the enemy's strong places. We destroy men's arguments. And we destroy every proud thing that raises itself against the knowledge of God. We capture every thought and make it give up and obey Christ.

2 CORINTHIANS 10:3-5

2 Corinthians

Taking Captives

Look around you. What do you see? Can you see the enemy trying to attack you? Do you see arrows flying across the room? Do you hear any machine guns?

No. God says our battle is just as strong as any you might see on TV. But the war we are fighting can't always be seen with our eyes or heard with our ears.

In fact, most battles happen right in our own minds. Satan and our own sin tempt us to trust ourselves more than God. The devil tells us lies all the time to try to trip us up and wound our faith in Jesus. To fight back, we have to know what God really says. We must have his truth hidden in our hearts. God's Word is the weapon we can use to fight Satan's lies.

Salvation

Then when we begin to hear Satan's lies in our minds, we can take those wrong thoughts captive. We tell ourselves God's truth. Each time we think more like Jesus, Satan falls back in defeat.

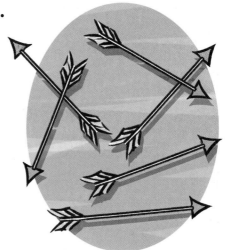

I must not become too proud of the wonderful things that were shown to me. So a painful problem was given to me. This problem is a messenger from Satan. It is sent to beat me and keep me from being too proud. I begged the Lord three times to take this problem away from me. But the Lord said to me, "My grace is enough for you. When you are weak, then my power is made perfect in you." So I am very happy to brag about my weaknesses. Then Christ's power can live in me. So I am happy when I have weaknesses, insults, hard times, sufferings, and all kinds of troubles. All these things are for Christ. And I am happy, because when I am weak, then I am truly strong.

2 CORINTHIANS 12:7-10

Weakest Link

Helmet of Salvation

Have you ever seen body builders on TV? It's hard to imagine how any person can get so strong. Even if they don't do it for sport, most guys want to be as strong as they can be.

Do you want to be strong? God says that if you want to be a strong warrior for Jesus, you first have to admit that you are weak! Of course, God is talking about your spiritual muscles.

239

He is talking about the kind of strength you need in order to do what he asks.

When we understand our weaknesses, we can ask God to be strong in us. He promises to fill us with his mighty Spirit. So it's not just eating healthy foods and exercising that make us strong. God gives us the power to do everything he asks us to do. He can do more through us than we can even imagine.

Salvation

ell God today that you need him to be your strength. Ask him to make you strong and powerful for his kingdom!

Those men who seemed to be important did not change the Good News that I preach. (It doesn't matter to me if they were "important" or not. To God all men are the same.) But these leaders saw that God had given me special work, just as he had to Peter. God gave Peter the work of telling the Good News to the Jews. But God gave me the work of telling the Good News to the non-Jewish people. God gave Peter the power to work as an apostle for the Jewish people. But he also gave me the power to work as an apostle for those who are not Jews. James, Peter, and John, who seemed to be the leaders, saw that God had given me this special grace. So they accepted Barnabas and me. They said, "Paul and Barnabas, we agree that you should go to the people who are not Jews. We will go to the Jews."

GALATIANS 2:6-9

Give Them a Hand

You're with your mom when she runs into some of her friends from church. She introduces you to them. You decide to:

A Stare at the ground and not say anything.

B Act bored and run off with a friend of your own.

C Smile a little and act shy.

D Look them in the eye, say "hello," and offer a handshake.

243

Grown-ups might make you feel shy or scared. After all, they are much bigger than you. But you don't need to be afraid! God says that every person in the body of Christ is important. It doesn't matter if you are big or small, young or old. God wants us to greet each other with joy and courage. He wants us to be courteous and polite to everyone—even grown-ups.

Heart

The next time you meet someone new, give them a strong handshake. Look them in the eye. Your bravery will make them feel noticed and important. It will also show them that you respect and value them as fellow brothers and sisters in Christ.

You heard the true teaching—the Good News about your salvation. When you heard it, you believed in Christ. And in Christ, God put his special mark on you by giving you the Holy Spirit that he had promised. That Holy Spirit is the guarantee that we will get what God promised for his people. This will bring full freedom to the people who belong to God, to bring praise to God's glory.

That is why I always remember you in my prayers and always thank God for you. I have always done this since the time I heard about your faith in the

Lord Jesus and your love for all God's people. I always pray to the God of our Lord Jesus Christ—to the glorious Father. I pray that he will give you a spirit that will make you wise in the knowledge of God—the knowledge that he has shown you. I pray that you will have greater under-standing in your heart. Then you will know the hope that God has chosen to give us. I pray that you will know that the blessings God has promised his holy people are rich and glorious. And you will know that God's power is very great for us who believe.

EPHESIANS 1:13-19

Time to Enlist

Helmet of Salvation

When a soldier enlists in the army, how many times does he have to sign up? Do you think that he signs up every day? Is he afraid the army won't want him anymore?

As God's mighty warriors, we don't need to ask Jesus to come into our hearts every day. If we have asked him to forgive us of our sin and take control of our lives, he does just that. God gives us his Spirit as a promise that he will keep his word.

God will never leave us or kick us out of his family. He wants us to act and think like the soldiers and children of God that we are. Whenever we choose to do right and love others, we show that God's Spirit is alive and working in us.

If you have never asked Jesus to be your Savior, now is the perfect time. Give your life to Jesus, and join the family of God's greatest warriors.

Salvation

I am in prison because I belong to the Lord. God chose you to be his people. I tell you now to live the way God's people should live. Always be humble and gentle. Be patient and accept each other with love. You are joined together with peace through the Spirit. Do all you can to continue together in this way. Let peace hold you together. There is one body and one Spirit. And God called you to have one hope. There is one Lord, one faith, and one baptism. There is one God and Father of everything. He rules everything. He is everywhere and in everything.

EPHESIANS 4:1-6

Peace Talks:
Wearing the Belt of Peace

When American soldiers go overseas to fight our enemies, they go as a group. They work together to fight the bad guys. But what would happen if they got confused? What would happen if they fought each other instead?

God wants his soldiers to be peacemakers. We are to work together to fight against evil. But stay alert!

Belt of Truth

The enemy wants to confuse us. He wants us to fight with our brothers and sisters in Christ.

Don't fall into his trap. Help to keep the peace in your home, school and church. Look for ways to build each other up instead of tearing each other down.

Truth

ACTIVITY

Work with a sibling or parent. Use blocks to build a high tower. The job of the other person is to tear it down. How high can you get? Now try again, with both of you working together. Did it grow higher? Likewise, God's kingdom will grow bigger and stronger when we work together to defeat evil.

You must stop telling lies. Tell each other the truth because we all belong to each other in the same body. When you are angry, do not sin. And do not go on being angry all day. Do not give the devil a way to defeat you. If a person is stealing, he must stop stealing and start working. He must use his hands for doing something good. Then he will have something to share with those who are poor.

When you talk, do not say harmful things. But say what people need—words that will help others become stronger. Then what you say will help those who listen to you. And do not make the Holy Spirit sad. The Spirit is God's proof that you belong to him. God gave you the Spirit to show that God will make you free when the time comes. Do not be bitter or angry or mad. Never shout angrily or say things to hurt others. Never do anything evil. Be kind and loving to each other. Forgive each other just as God forgave you in Christ.

EPHESIANS 4:25-32

Ephesians

Stay Sharp

Helmet of Salvation

Everyone has habits. A habit is anything you do over and over again. You can have good habits, like brushing your teeth before bed. Or you can have bad habits, like arguing with your parents.

God wants his warriors to develop the habit of listening to his Spirit. Every child of God has God's Spirit inside. His Spirit makes us feel joy when we are obeying the Lord. But when we disobey, the Holy Spirit makes us feel uncomfortable.

He reminds us that we are about to make a bad decision.

Be careful. If we ignore him over and over again, we stop hearing his voice. We don't feel as bad about our sin. Our hearts grow cold, and our friendship with God is hurt.

Don't let it happen! Ask God today to help you obey his Spirit inside you. Turn away from any sin you know that might be keeping you from growing in Jesus. Then develop the healthy habit of hearing and obeying God's Spirit.

Salvation

Children, obey your parents the way the Lord wants. This is the right thing to do. The command says, "Honor your father and mother." This is the first command that has a promise with it. The promise is: "Then everything will be well with you, and you will have a long life on the earth."

EPHESIANS 6:1-3

Ephesians

Think Tank

Shield of Faith

Aren't army tanks cool? With heavy armor all around, they seem to be able to roll almost anywhere. They're one of the best ways to avoid injury from enemy fire, and they pack a powerful punch, to boot.

Did you know that God has given you your own army tank for protection? Your parents act as protection, just like an armored tank.

God has hand picked your parents to train you to become a man of God. Your duty as a kid is to follow their instructions.

When you obey your parents, you are safe in your God-given tank. You have more power to shoot the enemy down. But when you choose to go your own way, you are leaving God's protection behind. Suddenly, you are an easy target.

Faith

Satan is always looking for Christians who have lowered their safety shields so he can hurt them. Don't let it happen to you. Stay safe and strong under your parents' shelter. Thank God for his perfect protection for you.

Does your life in Christ give you strength? Does his love comfort you? Do we share together in the Spirit? Do you have mercy and kindness? If so, you make me very happy by having the same thoughts, sharing the same love, and having one mind and purpose. When you do things, do not let selfishness or pride be your guide. Be humble and give more honor to others than to yourselves. Do not be interested only in your own life, but be interested in the lives of others.

PHILIPPIANS 2:1-4

Philippians

Open-Door Policy

You are walking into a restaurant at the same time as another family. You should:

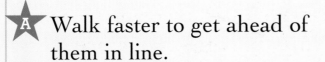

A Walk faster to get ahead of them in line.

B Squeeze through the door at the same time.

C Stand there and stare at them.

D Open the door for them to pass through.

If you're really hungry, it might be extra hard. But if you want to act like the good soldier you are, your good manners should come first. To hold the door open for other people lets them know you think they are important. It gives them honor and shows them just how much you love God. And it helps you learn how to serve others, as well as grow in patience.

Heart

Remember that, even though Jesus was God, he came to earth to serve. He always put our needs first. He tells his soldiers to act the same way he did. But don't worry. Your patience and kindness will be rewarded. Your family will be seated and eating in no time, too.

You were raised from death with Christ. So aim at what is in heaven, were Christ is sitting at the right hand of God. Think only about the things in heaven, not the things on earth. Your old sinful self has died, and your new life is kept with Christ in God. Christ is your life. When he comes again, you will share in his glory.

COLOSSIANS 3:1-4

Colossians

Heaven Help Us

Helmet of Salvation

When you picture heaven in your mind, what do you see? Maybe you think of gold streets. Angels. Lots of light and smiling faces. Jesus.

Thinking of heaven brings good thoughts to mind. It makes us remember the hope we have. We know that one day we will get to really go there and see it for ourselves.

God says that he also wants us to see it now, in our minds. He wants us to think about heavenly things. We need to remember what is important to Jesus. We must focus on our heavenly Father and remember what he says in his Word.

Do you sometimes forget that God is real? Do you start to think the world around you is all there is?

Salvation

Ask God now to help you remember the truth. Ask him to help you think heavenly thoughts all your days here on earth!

Continue praying and keep alert. And when you pray, always thank God. Also pray for us. Pray that God will give us an opportunity to tell people his message. Pray that we can preach the secret truth that God has made known about Christ. I am in prison because I preach this truth. Pray that I can speak in a way that will make it clear as I should.

Be wise in the way you act with people who are not believers. Use your time in the best way you can. When you talk, you should always be kind and wise. Then you will be able to answer everyone in the way you should.

Colossians

COLOSSIANS 4:2-6

Mind the Mines

Stand Strong

You were so excited! Kids from your neighborhood were getting together for a game of kickball. Not long into the game, you noticed some of the boys cheating. They even lied about an out, and it cost your team a score.

When people sin against us, it often makes us very angry. We want things to be made right. But God says to watch out!

If we get angry or take revenge, we may be making an even bigger problem. We might miss the chance to show God's love to others by our actions.

God wants us to always act in love and kindness, so others can see God in us. If we give in to our tempers, we don't look any different from the kids who don't trust Christ.

Strong

We need to use every chance we get to share God's truth in love, so others may know him, too. Ask God for wisdom and patience to share his Good News with the people around you.

Do the best you can to be the kind of person that God will approve, and give yourself to him. Be a worker who is not ashamed of his work—a worker who uses the true teaching in the right way. Stay away from those who talk about useless worldly things. That kind of talk will lead a person more and more away from God. Their evil teaching will spread like a sickness inside the body. Hymenaeus and Philetus are men like that. They have left the true teaching. They say that the rising from death of all men has already taken place. And those two men are destroying the faith of some people. But God's strong foundation continues to stand. These words are written on that foundation: "The Lord knows those who belong to him." And also these words are written on that foundation, "Everyone who says that he believes in the Lord must stop doing wrong."

2 TIMOTHY 2:15-19

2 Timothy

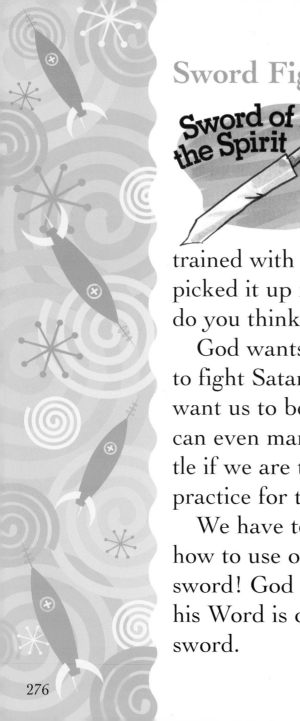

Sword Fight

Sword of the Spirit

Imagine a sword fight between two strong men. Only one of them is trained with a sword. The other just picked it up for the first time. Who do you think will win?

God wants his soldiers to be ready to fight Satan and sin. He doesn't want us to be taken by surprise. We can even march confidently into battle if we are trained. So how can we practice for the fight?

We have to learn how to use our sword! God says his Word is our sword.

When we know what the Bible says, we can use his truth to cut down the enemy's lies. But we will never know God's truth if we don't study his Word. If we don't memorize it, we will forget our sword the moment we need it most.

Ask God today to help you become the best swordsman you can be! Then start sharpening your sword skills as you memorize his Word.

Mind Guard

HEBREWS 4:12

God's word is alive and working. It is sharper than a sword sharpened on both sides. It cuts all the way into us, where the soul and the spirit are joined. It cuts to the center of our joints and our bones. And God's word judges the thoughts and feelings in our hearts.

You should continue following the teachings that you learned. You know that these teachings are true. And you know you can trust those who taught you. You have known the Holy Scriptures since you were a child. The Scriptures are able to make you wise. And that wisdom leads to salvation through faith in Christ Jesus. All Scripture is inspired by God and is useful for teaching and for showing people what is wrong in their lives. It is useful for correcting faults and teaching how to live right. Using the Scriptures, the person who serves God will be ready and will have everything he needs to do every good work.

2 TIMOTHY 3:14-17

2 Timothy

You've Got Mail

Sword of the Spirit

Have you ever been to a library?

Thousands of books line the shelves. Each has a different title and story. With so many books in the world, why do Christians care so much about the Bible?

The Bible is different from any other book ever written. It's the only book God himself wrote. He chose to write it using people who listened to his Holy Spirit.

He filled their minds with his thoughts. He wrote the words, using their hands. The Bible is like a letter from God written to his people.

God's Word is perfectly true. It doesn't have any lies or fake stories in it, because God doesn't lie.

Spirit

When we study the Bible, we are learning exactly what God thinks and feels about us. We need to know what God says if we want to know him in truth. Ask Jesus to speak to you today through his Word.

Mind Guard

2 TIMOTHY 3:16

All Scripture is inspired by God
and is useful for teaching and for showing
people what is wrong in their lives.
It is useful for correcting
faults and teaching how to
live right.

In the past God spoke to our ancestors through the prophets. He spoke to them many times and in many different ways. And now in these last days God has spoken to us through his Son. God has chosen his Son to own all things. And he made the world through the Son. The Son reflects the glory of God. He is an exact copy of God's nature. He holds everything together with his powerful word. The Son made people clean from their sins. Then he sat down at the right side of God, the Great One in heaven. The Son became much greater than the angels. And God gave him a name that is much greater than theirs.

HEBREWS 1:1-4

The Fiercest Fighter: Jesus

Have you ever seen a sponge with a scrubber on one side? One side is soft for wiping, and the other is rough to scratch off dirt. Did you know that Jesus has some of the same qualities?

The softer side of Jesus is patient, loving and kind. He cares for the sick and needy and was willing to die to save us from our sins.

Often when we think of him, we see him smiling and gentle—but we do not see him as a warrior.

Jesus is not only soft and gentle; he is also tough and strong. He is the fiercest fighter of evil. With wisdom and power he created the universe. He has declared war against sin and death. When he rose from the dead, he defeated the powers of hell.

Warriors

We need to be aware of who Jesus really is when we worship him. Take time now to think about his awesome power. Then praise him for both his strength and love.

Brothers, we are completely free to enter the Most Holy Place. We can do this without fear because of the blood of Jesus' death. We can enter through a new way that Jesus opened for us. It is a living way. It leads through the curtain—Christ's body. And we have a great priest over God's house. So let us come near to God with a sincere heart and a sure faith. We have been cleansed and made free from feelings of guilt. And our bodies have been washed with pure water. Let us hold firmly to the hope that we have confessed. We can trust God to do what he promised.

HEBREWS 10:19-23

Friends in High Places

If you had a problem, would you ask the President of the United States for help? Probably not. You imagine he's too busy. Too important. He wouldn't even know who you are.

Unless he was your dad. If you were the president's son, you could talk to him whenever. You could ask him anything. And he'd have the power to help you.

Helmet of Salvation

287

The Bible says that you have someone even more important than the president as your Father. God himself has adopted you into his family. You are his child, and he loves for you to come to him. He is never too busy or too important for you. He delights for you to tell him all about your day and to ask him for help whenever you need it. He is always there for you.

Salvation

Take a moment now to thank your heavenly Father for wanting you to be in his family. Then tell him whatever you want. Rest easy, knowing he loves to hear from you and help you.

It was by faith Abraham obeyed God's call to go to another place that God promised to give him. He left his own country, not knowing where he was to go. It was by faith that he lived in the country God promised to give him. He lived there like a visitor who did not belong. He lived in tents with Isaac and Jacob, who had received that same promise from God. Abraham was waiting for the city that has real foundations—the city planned and built by God.

He was too old to have children, and Sarah was not able to have children. It was by faith that Abraham was made able to become a father. Abraham trusted God to do what he had promised. This man was so old that he was almost dead. But from him came as many descendants as there are stars in the sky. They are as many as the grains of sand on the seashore that cannot be counted.

HEBREWS 11:8-12

Hebrews

Fall Back, Men!:
Wearing the Belt of Faith

God's people weren't cowards. They had to fight hard to share the Good News. Many were killed because of their faith.

Why were they willing to lose everything for Jesus? They knew that Jesus was more important than anything here on earth. They knew Jesus would take care of them here and in heaven.

God says that we can't please him if we don't have faith.

Our work as his children is to believe what God says. If you have trouble trusting God, don't worry. Just ask God to help you believe his word, and he will increase your faith.

ACTIVITY

Want to practice faith? Have your parent (not your sibling) stand behind you. When they say "go," close your eyes and fall backward, with arms reaching outward. Trust them to catch you before you fall. Like faith in God, it is a scary exercise. But the person you trust is good. Like God, they will not let you down!

Through Jesus let us always offer our sacrifice to God. This sacrifice is our praise, coming from lips that speak his name. Do not forget to do good to others. And share with them what you have. These are the sacrifices that please God.

Obey your leaders and be under their authority. These men are watching you because they are responsible for your souls. Obey them so that they will do this work with joy, not sadness. It will not help you to make their work hard.

Continue praying for us. We feel sure about what we are doing, because we always want to do the right thing.

HEBREWS 13:15-18

Hebrews

Basic Training

Shield of Faith

Good soldiers who rise in the ranks quickly know how to listen. They don't disobey orders. They even learn to think like a good soldier. Soon they don't need to be told what to do. They know what is right, and they do it.

Have you ever wondered why your mom and dad tell you what to do?

Your parents and teachers are training you to be a good soldier. They teach you the right way to think and act. God says that if you respect them, you will be a better soldier. You will be smarter and wiser than kids who disobey. As you grow older, you will be thankful for the training you had when you were young. You will know what is God's way and choose it, even with no one around to tell you what to do.

Faith

Do you have trouble obeying? Ask God to change your heart. Tell him and your leaders that you are thankful for their training.

Do what God's teaching says; do not just listen and do nothing. When you only sit and listen, you are fooling yourselves. A person who hears God's teaching and does nothing is like a man looking in a mirror. He sees his face, then goes away and quickly forgets what he looked like. But the truly happy person is the one who carefully studies God's perfect law that makes people free. He continues to study it. He listens to God's teaching and does not forget what he heard. Then he obeys what God's teaching says. When he does this, it makes him happy.

JAMES 1:22-25

Taking Orders

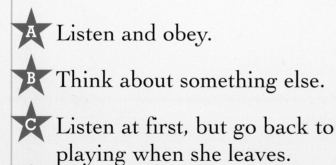

Your mom is telling you for the third time to clean your room. Then she starts to repeat why keeping clean is important. You decide to:

A Listen and obey.

B Think about something else.

C Listen at first, but go back to playing when she leaves.

D Argue why you shouldn't have to clean your room.

Do you ever get tired of being told what to do? Jesus knows his warriors often struggle to do what's right. So he reminds us how to do it.

Doing what is right requires two things. First, you must listen to instruction. Stop talking, playing, or doing other things when a parent or teacher is speaking to you.

Heart

After hearing, get up and obey right away. Don't wait, or you might forget.

When your parent asks you to do something you don't want to do, don't worry. Fight the sin in your heart with a prayer to God asking for help. He will give you the strength you need to listen and obey.

Is there anyone among you who is truly wise and understanding? Then he should show his wisdom by living right. He should do good things without being proud. A wise person does not brag. But if you are selfish and have bitter jealousy in your hearts, you have no reason to brag. Your bragging is a lie that hides the truth. That kind of "wisdom" does not come from God. That "wisdom" comes from the world. It is not spiritual. It is from the devil. Where there is jealousy and selfishness, there will be confusion and every kind of evil. But the wisdom that comes from God is like this: First, it is pure. Then it is also peaceful, gentle, and easy to please. This wisdom is always ready to help those who are troubled and to do good for others. This wisdom is always fair and honest. When people work for peace in a peaceful way, they receive the good result of their right-living.

JAMES 3:13-18

Bragging Rights

Do you like to hear others tell you how smart or fast or strong they think they are? Why do you think it bothers you?

Unfortunately, all of us are sinners. We often like to think that we got our good looks or good gifts on our own. Then we brag about it. We want to make our friends wish they had the same talents or toys.

The truth is that every good thing about us comes from God. He gave them all to us.

Helmet of Salvation

What we own, and even how our bodies are made, have nothing to do with us. All glory and thanks goes to God!

When we brag to others, we are taking credit from God and giving it to ourselves. God says that is foolish. He says we need to be wise. We must remember the true Giver. Take time today to thank God for making you the way he did. Ask him to help you remember that your gifts come from him.

Salvation

Younger men should be willing to be under older men. And all of you should be very humble with each other.

"God is against the proud, but he gives grace to the humble." *Proverbs 3:34*

So be humble under God's powerful hand. Then he will lift you up when the right time comes. Give all your worries to him, because he cares for you.

1 PETER 5:5-7

1 Peter

Super Strength:
Wearing the Belt of Obedience

What do you do when you want to show how tough you are? Do you flex your muscles? Do you yell at the top of your lungs?

God's warriors are supposed to be strong men. But God's strength doesn't show up the way we might think. God says that we need to know our place.

Younger men and boys are to listen and obey the teachers in their lives. It's hard to admit that we are weak and need help, but it's the truth. When we are willing to let God teach us through those in authority over us, we honor God. We honor our parents. And we grow stronger and wiser each time we obey.

Truth

ACTIVITY

Practice flexing your muscles. How many push-ups can you do? How many sit-ups? Were you tired after exercising? God never gets tired because he is all-powerful. Ask God to make you a strong soldier by giving you a heart that obeys his Word.

Here is the message we have heard from God and now tell to you: God is light, and in him there is no darkness at all. So if we say that we have fellowship with God, but we continue living in darkness, then we are liars. We do not follow the truth. God is in the light. We should live in the light, too. If we live in the light, we share fellowship with each other. And when we live in the light, the blood of the death of Jesus, God's Son, is making us clean from every sin.

If we say that we have no sin, we are fooling ourselves, and the truth is not in us. But if we confess our sins, he will forgive our sins. We can trust God. He does what is right. He will make us clean from all the wrongs we have done. If we say that we have not sinned, then we make God a liar. We do not accept God's true teaching.

1 JOHN 1:5-10

Boot-Camp Blunders

Helmet of Salvation

Did you know that even the best soldiers have to go through training? Not one man can get around it. They learn skills through exercises.. When they fail, they learn what not to do. Then they get up and practice again.

As God's mighty warrior, you are in training, too. God uses the people and events in your life to shape you into a better son and soldier.

He knows you aren't perfect, so there is no need to act like you are. Whenever you sin, don't hide it. You won't learn or get stronger if you pretend you don't need help. Instead, be brave and tell God what you did wrong. You need to admit it to a person if you wronged them, too. Then ask God to forgive you and help you make better choices.

Salvation

God promises to forgive you every time. He also gives you the strength to fight sin better the next time.

My dear friends, many false prophets are in the world now. So do not believe every spirit. But test the spirits to see if they are from God.

. . . My dear children, you belong to God. So you have defeated them because God's Spirit, who is in you, is greater than the devil, who is in the world.

1 JOHN 4:1, 4

1 John

Secret Weapons

Shield of Faith

What is your weapon of choice? Do you like to swing your sword like a brave knight? Do you pretend to shoot Indians like a cowboy? As a soldier in God's army, you count on him to supply you with the weapons you need to fight the enemy.

God's secret weapons can't be seen with your eyes. First, he gives us his own Holy Spirit inside our hearts. God's Spirit who is in us is greater and more powerful than the devil who is in the world. The Spirit prays for us, strengthens us and guides us. Besides the Holy Spirit, God also gives us angels to protect us throughout the day.

Faith

sk God today to help you remember your spiritual weapons. Then rely on each one to help you be a better and stronger soldier for Jesus.

Prayer Requests

Prayer Requests

Answered Prayers

Answered Prayers

Answered Prayers